Praise for Customer Ad Care, People

"Great customer service is hard to come by in today's world of 'faster, not better.' In *Customer Advocacy,* Nicolette Wuring proves great customer service is the key to creating growth through consumer-led promotion, loyalty, and peer-to-peer recommendations. *Customer advocacy* is high trust in action, increasing speed and lowering costs. Set yourself apart—care!"

--Stephen M. R. Covey, *New York Times* bestselling author of *The Speed of Trust: The One Thing That Changes Everything*

"In *Customer Advocacy,* Nicolette Wuring shows the vital importance of making real connections with customers. She does this brilliantly by giving both very practical and effective recommendations and profound conceptual insights."

--Wessel Ganzevoort, Boardroom consultant for Leadership and Organization and Professor at the Amsterdam Business School (University of Amsterdam)

"Wake up! Growth fetish nearly made us believe business isn't about love but preferences. It's not about people but FTE's, not about customers but RGU's (revenue generating units). Well, guess what, in *Customer Advocacy,* Nicolette Wuring shows us it is a dead end street. In a world where nothing is truly original anymore, authentic customer care is magic! Great to give, fantastic to receive. It makes our day! So ask yourself: is your brand ready to make the day?

--Jenny Elissen, Founding Partner NewGenes, Business innovation network

Customer Advocacy
When You Care, People Notice

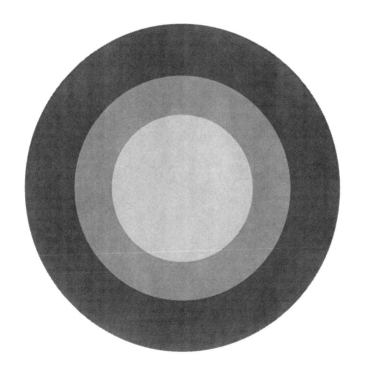

Nicolette Wuring

Table of Contents

Acknowledgements

A special thank you goes out to all the people who inspired me: my mentors, especially Paula Sullivan, Jenny Elissen, Wessel Ganzevoort, Lou Carbone, Stephen M.R. Covey, Gene Musselman; my parents; my sisters; my friends; and all the authors of all those books I read, especially during my work life. Your wisdom, your support, and the mirrors you held up for me to challenge and confront me have been and are crucial to me on my path of personal and professional growth. Thank you. May people like you cross my path until the day I die. I dedicate this book to all of you.

Having a vision is one thing, being able to try and test it on multiple occasions are gifts, but writing a book about it that is fun and easy to read is something else. I would like to thank the people who contributed to getting my book into shape: Marieke Strobbe, Isabella Ottens-Helmer, Jenny Elissen, Dirk Devos, Anne Marie van Benthum and all those others who contributed their reviews and comments that helped shape this book.

Introduction

"When you care, people notice." Ever since I can remember, these words have been my point of reference in everything I've done. First, I was a pleaser. I set out to make other people like me, so I pretended to care. More recently, I realized that when I do the things I care about, instead of pretending, care becomes an energizing principle. Pretending to care costs a lot of energy. Doing things I care about creates a lot of energy. And, I achieve much better results than I ever could have imagined. The beauty of it is, I found out that this works the same in business.

Care (I can hear some of you thinking) *this is not the kind of word to use in a business book, especially not so prominently.* Well, let me warn you now. By the time you finish reading this book, you will not only understand why it's being used and start using it, too, but you may choose to start doing the things you care about and to enable the people who work for you (or, as you may come to think, the people you work with) to do it, too. When you care, the people who are your employees and your customers will notice, and they will reward you(-r company) with their advocacy, becoming ambassadors for your organization.

When the people in a company pretend to care, they know they are being hypocritical. They find themselves under the constant threat of being found out. Managing that fear costs a lot of energy, which is therefore not being invested in achieving the goals of their employer. When the people in a company are (en-)able(-d) to do the things they care about, they have a lot more energy to spend on "the right things" (the things that matter), and that gives them, and the company they work for, wings—results they and the company never could have imagined.

When a company pretends to care, but actually is only interested in the results it reports to its shareholders, it spends a lot of energy pretending. Because top management sets the tone, everybody in that environment does the same. That's how unwritten rules and company politics come into being. However, what I have experienced is that when I create an environment where people are open and honest about the things they care about (including the interests of the shareholders—let's face it, a business is in business to make money), it drives the sting out of a fear-driven culture. It makes unwritten rules and company politics useless. Enabling the people in a company to do the things they care about creates a lot more energy, soon they're reporting results that exceed everyone's expectations.

For example: my work with UPC Broadband, an over ten million customer multi-system (cable) operator in eleven countries in Europe. I was responsible for the turnaround of the reputation of the company's customer-facing side from worst in class to best, winning two Contact Center Awards and a nomination for the Customer Relationship Management (CRM) Award with the Pan European CRM case. Service is now one of the key differentiators of UPC Broadband; the cost to serve, the operational efficiency, and the customer acquisition costs decreased materially; the employee and customer advocacy as well as the share of wallet; the reputation, value, and competitiveness of the brand; and, all in all, profitability increased significantly and the share price soared.

The secret of success here is not what I did. It's what the people in that organization did! All I did is change the environment for the people in the organization in such a way that people can start to do the things they like and care about. The energy and creativity but also the accountability that is created makes these transformations successful; therefore, it is their success. I am humbled by their successes.

I wrote this book because it is my passion to assist, guide and inspire companies in their strategic reorientation and transformation from being product-driven to people- and customer-driven, from shareholder-driven to stakeholder-driven, making companies great environments for people to work and great partners with which to do business.

My dream is that every organization becomes a great environment.

Whether you are a marketer, in sales, in customer service, responsible for PR, for HR, for business strategy or the CEO of a company, you will increasingly have found yourself come across terminology like Attraction Economy, Expectation Economy, Return on Involvement, Emotional Age, Customer Experience, Customer Dialogue, Customer Loyalty, maybe even Customer Advocacy, or Net Promoter Score, Detractors, Neutrals and Promoters. You probably found yourself wondering, is this the next hype? Why would I need to concern myself with this? If you find yourself in a position within a company where part of your concern is the differentiating power of your business, competitiveness of your business, profitable and organic growth of your business, retention, 'share of wallet', brand value, brand reputation, etc., this book is a must read.

I hope that this book will contribute to this dream by its sharing with you in a very personal and pragmatic way how I approach these kinds of transformational processes. I hope that this book will inspire you, will spark your creativity, and will challenge you to take ownership and responsibility for what happens in the workplace with you and the people you work with.

Note: When I use "he" in this book, I mean he or she interchangeably. When I talk about "company," this can fit any organizational situation you have in mind.

Also, there will be cases where you may want to distinguish between 'brand' and 'company'. In some cases the two will be the same, in others companies may use different brands for different segments. When pursuing customer advocacy as a strategy, the approach depends on how much the two are connected. The closer a separate brand is connected to the 'corporate brand', the more the 'separate brand' will be impacted by its 'corporate brand'. So, where I use the words brand or company, it's up to you, as a reader, to define what is applicable for the case you have in mind.

Customer Advocacy

With customer advocacy, the customer is the originator and the motive is essentially selfless. You can't pay a customer a premium to become an advocate for your business. It's something that is driven by how a company makes a customer feel about himself, which reflects on how he feels about a company.

C AN YOU REMEMBER the last time you recommended a company to your family and friends? Think about the last typical social event you attended. At some point, the conversation must have hit the subject of a company someone had a positive or negative customer experience with. Take, for instance, a telecom provider, a bank, or a grocery store. Remember the person talking about his experiences with the company. Remember the people who added stories about their own experiences with that company. How did these stories, good or bad, impact your own feelings about and behavior with respect to that company?

We are customers every day. I challenge you to go back to your own experiences and ask yourself, Have I ever been an advocate by actively promoting a company to my family and friends? How did I feel when I did so? What is it that made me do it? What was my behavior when I felt that way? Am I still a customer of that company? If not, why not? Customer advocacy is not high level. It's very down-to-earth, and we all have felt or feel it—or not.

An Advocate, Me?

In this book, I deliberately opted not to discuss best practices for customer advocacy at large multinational companies. Why? Because there aren't a lot of good examples out there yet. That is, in the brick-and-mortar world. However, the companies that became multinational rapidly over the last, say, ten years in the online world (such as Amazon, eBay, and Google) are excellent examples. These are the kinds of companies that built and grew their business based on advocacy. The sheer fact that they are online companies means that they are ruled by the ethic of the online world. That ethic implies that they can only grow their business when they are positively recommended in the online world by their customers (peer-to-peer). Their reputation in the online world is decisive for the success of their business.

A brilliant example that portrays the simplicity of creating customer advocacy can be found on the Web in a four-minute movie, The Simple Truths of Service (www. stservicemovie.com). This clip is based on a small book by Barbara Glanz and Ken Blanchard[1]. I highly recommend that you take a look at it and let it sink in.

To make it more practical, let me try to help you feel it more. Following, I will describe advocacy from three different perspectives: you as a customer, you as an employee, and "you" as the product that is being "sold."

YOU AS A CUSTOMER

Imagine you are a Dutch citizen living in the Netherlands, who wrote a book in US English, aimed at the global business community. You want to publish your book so it will find its way to the audience you are targeting. You have no experience in publishing books, let alone a book in English for a global audience, so where do you start? You think about your own behavior when you want to buy a book. You probably go online and search on Amazon. You do some research on the Web, to find out about experiences from other people who once found themselves in the same situation. You use Google and research the results. You read people's comments on the subject in blogs. You ask around in your network. You meet with some people who have already been published.

You decide to explore an online self-publishing company. But which do you pick? You're bound to pick one that is connected to a company you already know and have experience with as a customer, i.e., the self-publishing company Amazon has under its wings, BookSurge. Though you don't know anyone personally who has experience with BookSurge, you read what other authors have to say on their blogs. And, of course, you have your own experiences with Amazon. As a last step, you research the company, its mission, and its core values. You like what you read. It all makes you feel like BookSurge could be the right company to help you get your book on the market.

You're a little lazy. It looks like all information you need is on their Website, but rather than plowing your way through it, you decide to send them an email, because you'd like to talk with a real person. So, you send an email to BookSurge through their Website, asking for more information. (Note: Although I did publish this book using BookSurge, the story that follows is 50% fictional, because in order for the book to be published, the manuscript had to be ready, and as of this writing the manuscript is not ready yet! The names of the people are fictitious.)

The next day you receive a reply from a gentleman introducing himself as Bob. Bob's personal contact details are in the email, and he informs you that he's going to be there for you all the way through what is for you a new experience, to guide you and advise you. He has added a short questionnaire to his email, and asks you to fill it out. You do so and send it back to him the same day. Then, it's quiet for a week, until you receive an email from Bob checking to see if you received his prior email because he hasn't heard back from you yet. That's funny, but you're glad he contacts you. So you re-send your previous email, and within a day Bob gets back to you to set up an international call to discuss with you how his company can serve you. At the agreed time, you're still in a meeting that is running late. You miss your appointment with Bob. He leaves you a voicemail and emails you to propose another time for the next day. The next day you're available, and Bob gets through to you.

Bob starts the conversation with you. He shows sincere interest in your book. The first fifteen minutes of the conversation are spent talking about you and your book. Bob listens, and the conversation is off to an enthusiastic start. Then Bob starts with stipulating that he wants to do everything he can to make your book a success. He talks you through the process and how he and his company will help you each step of the way, from editing, formatting and cover design, to marketing and public relations for your book. You will have a professional editor assigned to you and a graphic design team, who will support you in this process. You will be set up by Bob personally, over the phone, with your own online account, so you can manage, review, and comment on all the work the teams in the U.S. do for you each step of the way. All through the process he will be there for you as your personal adviser to guide you smoothly through the process. Your book will be registered with an ISBN number by his company, which will make it easy to find for more traditional channels like bookstores. Your book will be sold through Amazon, he says, so people will have the customer experience they are used to on Amazon even though it's on-demand printing. Since you wrote a business book, that's pretty convenient, because your potential readers are members of the global business community. That's why you wrote your book in English.

Bob makes it explicit that he is looking for your input and feedback to create a package for you that fits your needs. He ends the conversation with the remark that he will send you an overview of the options he thinks will be relevant for you based on your conversation with him. He suggests an appointment for the following week to discuss further and give you time to digest the information he will send you so you don't have to take the time to figure it all out from their Website. He is making it easy for you.

Shortly after this first conversation, you receive the email containing the information Bob promised you. Every email you receive from Bob (and his colleagues later in the process) ends with a question: "How's my driving? Did this answer appropriately address your question(s)?" This question is followed by two hyperlinks, one for "yes" and one for "no." That question, combined with the personal communication he had with you so far, creates a feeling about him and the company he represents. What feeling do you get so far?

In his email, Bob follows each step of the process as discussed, with hyperlinks to the relevant material on their Website. Following the hyperlinks, you land on pages that are easy to print, so you can have a closer look and read it through carefully. There's also a link to an application that guides you in the selection of the options that you decide are applicable to you, adds the time needed, the costs involved, calculates the minimum retail price and the royalties you will make on your book.

So, after studying all materials, you follow the link to the mentioned application and you do the math. The disadvantage of self-publishing is that you need to make all the investment yourself, instead of a publisher who pays you an upfront fee to publish and market it for you. But, especially in Europe, many publishers are nationally focused, and you want your book available for the global business and marketing community. The required investment is reasonable, so you decide to go ahead with the online self-publishing company.

The following week Bob calls you, as agreed. A couple of days before the call, you emailed Bob all the questions you have after reading the materials he sent you and doing the math. Bob clearly has studied all your questions and comes to the call well-prepared. He informs you that he will send you the answers in writing also after the call. After going through all your questions and Bob's satisfactory answers, you decide to go ahead and publish your book using his company. Bob is obviously thrilled about your decision. The process starts. He talks you through the manuscript submission specifications (which he will also send you) so you can get your manuscript ready to send it to the editor. Since you are a non-native English speaker and this is your first book, the first step in the process will be an editorial evaluation of your manuscript by a professional editor who will assess the content of your document. Bob informs you how and when he will set you up with your own account on their Website, where you can submit your manuscript, and what will be the working space for you and the people of his company involved in getting your book ready for publication.

At the agreed time and date, Bob calls you. It takes him about ten minutes to set up your personal account with him on their Website. You now have your own work space to work with the people from his company to get your book ready for publication. In addition, he informs you about the people who will support you. After the call, Bob sends you their names and short biographies by email. You also receive an email from Philip, who introduces himself as your editor. Philip expresses his excitement to be supporting you in the first phase of the process.

Using the manuscript submission specifications you received from Bob, you prepare your manuscript, submit it to your account, and although you know that this will trigger an alert to Philip automatically, you also send Philip an email to let him know your manuscript is now available for him to start work. You were informed that this step in the process would take about two weeks, which Philip confirms in his reply to you. Within twelve days, you receive an alert from Philip that he has reviewed your manuscript and that his feedback is ready for you to be viewed and processed. You also receive an email from Philip, in which he enthusiastically compliments you with your manuscript and lets you know that he's available for you by phone if you want to discuss his feedback with him in person.

You have a call with Philip to go through his feedback. You feel that he grasps the message you want to get across, and he is genuinely enthusiastic. His is open, honest, yet constructively critical at some points, and his feedback improves the flow of your manuscript and makes it even better. You put down the receiver, feeling excited about how things are progressing. You feel there's a good energy around it. It gives you trust for the future of your book.

You go to your account, process Philip's feedback in your manuscript and initiate the next phase. This is an exciting phase, because now you get to work with Thomas, the graphic designer, to design the cover of your book. Within hours you receive an email from Thomas. Thomas informs you that he is excited about working with you on this next phase. He paints the process for you, and suggests a call to discuss together how you want your book to look on the outside.

Well, I could go on, but let me ask you, how many "feel good moments" did you count while reading this paragraph? The way the people interact with you, their professionalism, their integrity, their authentic enthusiasm and care for your book, the way they communicate with you, manage your expectations, stick to their commitments to you, respond proactively and think ahead using their experience in the domain where you have none, along with their genuine care, makes you feel you can trust them and the company they represent. They literally take away the hassle (and anxiety) of getting your book published and make it a fun experience, that not only leads to a published book but also one that has become better than the manuscript with which you started. You believe it will sell more copies because of the way they all supported you.

Ask yourself, if you would have such experiences with a company, how would that make you feel? How would you talk about it to your family, friends, business partners, or on online social networks?

YOU AS AN EMPLOYEE

Thinking back to your initial research, you realize that in every interaction you had with the company so far, the people of the company have fully lived up to the expectations that were created by the mission and core values of the company. These people literally breathe and live the values. It is obvious that they love their job and the company for which they work.

Customer advocacy cannot exist without **Employee Advocacy**. Let's go back to Bob, Philip and Thomas in our example. How would you feel if you were one of them? About your job? About your company? How would you talk about the company with your family and friends? Picture yourself at a party, you know, the one where the questions go around: "What company do you work for?" and "What do you do for that company?" I bet when bad customer experiences are being exchanged and you know that the company you work for doesn't perform any better, you'd rather hold your tongue in silence than risking the next round of bad experience exchanges. But when you are proud of your company and you know your company creates good or even excellent customer experiences, you're bound to sit up straight, waiting for an opportunity to bring it up.

In your daily work, do you feel valued and respected? Do you feel autonomy with respect to the way you treat customers, be it internal or external? What about the values of the company? What about the purpose of your daily work? What do you feel about the environment in which you work? How about the people you work with (i.e., who report to you and to whom you report)?

'YOU' AS THE PRODUCT THAT IS BEING DELIVERED

Imagine you are the book (or the author) that is seeking to be published. How would it feel to know that you are going to be handled with care, by people who care about your success, who care about how good you will look, who care about you reaching the right audience and as many people across the globe as possible, so you can get your message out there? I think it would feel great!

CHAPTER 2

Customer Advocacy, the Next Competitive Battleground

Customer advocacy is the ultimate differentiator and the most sustainable one. The way a company makes its customers feel and its value as perceived by customers increasingly becomes decisive for the success of a company.

SINCE THE RISE of the World Wide Web, the voice of the customer has become so powerful that it has started to materially and undeniably impact the potential for success of companies, much like the talk in a small town village in the days before mass communication. Consumers are so connected that word-of-mouth, one-to-one influencing nowadays plays a bigger role than marketing communication. People increasingly judge and critique companies from the quality of their products and services to the consistency of their actual behavior compared to their marketing communication and corporate social responsibility claims. Virtual social networks spread the news faster and across larger geographic areas than any marketing message can be spread by companies themselves. When you don't care, people notice, and people tell it to the world in all kinds of online social communities—communities that reach consumers all over the world faster than traditional marketing messages, and with much more impact.

Not only has the voice of the customer become more powerful than traditional marketing communication, but the circumstances that define meaning and value to customers have also changed. Consumers nowadays are confronted with an abundance of choices. Products and services have become quite similar and so has quality. Prices are more often than not quite comparable. Consumers have so much choice that preferences and emotions have become crucial. The tangible attributes of a product have far less influence on consumer preference than subconscious sensory and emotional elements. The way a company makes customers feel and the value as perceived by a customer increasingly decides the success of a company.

The domains companies traditionally compete in are changing dramatically and rapidly. These changes erode the traditional competitive power of companies and undermine their customer relationships. Customer loyalty and retention are in every CEOs top ten list of challenges or greatest concerns.[2] Meanwhile, acquiring new customers is becoming more and more expensive, especially when customers are lost before having earned back the investment it took to acquire them in the first place. One of the few ways for organic growth companies have left is to grow the "share of wallet" of their existing customers. This requires a relationship with customers of trust and loyalty. As a result, customers will spend more, buy more, buy the company's other products, and recommend the company to their families and friends by spreading positive word-of-mouth.

It is against this background that companies can no longer afford to deal with customers only as efficiently and effectively as possible from the company's perspective. It's becoming more urgent to reconsider the "reason for being" of customers.

For decades, company strategies centered around operational excellence and product leadership. Companies have been forced to focus on the bottom line in order to please their shareholders. They have taken operational excellence to the limit. Product leadership has become a utopia in a world where the speed with which competitors (existing, completely new and unexpected ones) eat away any advantage companies thought they had faster than they can bring the next innovation to the market. Quality has become a prerequisite to be a player at all. Customer intimacy is often set aside as not feasible, both from an economic and an organizational point of view.

Consumers can no longer be fooled by clever campaigns if the actual customer experience doesn't match the created expectations. The perception of a brand and the emotional connection with it is growing in importance in the consumer choice process. Perception and connection are increasingly established by what other consumers say about a brand and their experiences with a company through word-of-mouth and online consumer-generated media. We've all at least heard of or even seen the videos that unsatisfied customers share on worldwide platforms such as YouTube.

Sustainable competitive advantages and the differentiating power of a brand in this day and age are moving towards being outside of a company's control. The quality of products and services along with operational excellence have become prerequisites to be a player at all. The competitive playing field is moving towards preference, commitment, and loyalty of customers.

Preference, commitment, and loyalty translates not only into customers who will remain customers, but who will also increase their spending with a company. In order to improve sustainable competitive advantages, de-commoditize products and services, and increase the differentiating power of a brand, in today's competitive playing field there needs to be significant customer advocacy.

Customer advocacy is not something that can be achieved systematically. With customer advocacy, the customer is the originator and the driver. The motive is driven by emotions and is essentially selfless. You can't pay a customer a premium to become an advocate for your business. It's something that is driven by how a company makes a customer feel about himself, which reflects on how he feels, and talks, about a company. A customer who recommends a company to his family and friends is authentic and requires authentic behavior in return from the company and its employees.

Customers: Generation Y

Dutch research executed in 2006[3] about the age group born after 1980 indicates that this generation bases its buying decisions on how authentic a company is. They are referred to in literature as *millennials*, *Generation Y* or the *gaming generation*. This generation bases its decision to play a game on the ethics displayed in a game. The ethics of a game are an important factor in deciding if they want to play. Ethics become a self-cleaning principle, creating behavior they carry over into the real world. The importance of the Generation Y as a customer base is growing. As consumers, they are savvy in dealing with the abundance of information and choice in today's world because they grew up with it. The choices they make are based on the ethics and the authenticity of a company. If they don't like it, they take their business to a competing company.

Customers: Generation BY

Of course, Generation Y is not the only generation you have to take into consideration. There are also the *Generations Before Generation Y* (Generations BY). Those are basically all generations born before Generation Y. Baby Boomers, Generation X, etc. Something interesting is happening with these generations as well. If you look at the increasing interest in spirituality in all shapes and forms among these generations and the growing concern for and interest in the environment, the ethics and authenticity of companies are increasingly becoming part of the way these generations assess companies as well. These generations have growing concerns and insecurities due to the rapid changes they are confronted with due to globalization, internationalization, digitalization, terrorism, digital crime —all the changes that are touching their world. On the one hand, this impacts their perception and assessment of companies; on the other hand, it offers interesting business opportunities for companies who are able to create trust with these generations by helping them address their concerns and insecurities.

Customers: Co-creators of Value
These developments force companies to reconsider their value propositions. As subconscious sensory and emotional elements become the focus of the value proposition, companies need to change the way they operate and transform and enlarge the customer's role.

Customers become co-creators of value, working towards common objectives in partnership with the company that is trying to serve their needs.

Customers base decisions on unconscious feelings. Ultimately, it's the way customers feel as a result of doing business with a company that reflects how they value a brand on an unconscious level. That's with what they become bonded. Customers value the reality they perceive and feel. It's not what customers feel about a company, but rather what customers feel about themselves when and as a result of interacting with a company. This changes the perspective, and forces companies to reconsider the value proposition they offer their customers. The overview below shows you how emotional the assessment of a value proposition of customers is from the perspectives of value, brand and relationship.[4] Out of the eight listed customer perceptions, there is only one that is rational—the perception of the balance between quality and price. Even that can be argued when one is, for instance, buying a car and choosing between a BMW and some other brand.

	Rational	Emotional
Value		
Perception of balance between quality and price	X	
Perception of convenience of doing business with a company		X
Brand		
Attitude towards brand		X
Perception of the ethics of a brand comparing to a customer's own ethics		X
Brand awareness		X
Relationship		
Perception of the strength of the relationship		X
Word-of-mouth; profiling in consumer-generated media		X
Preference, commitment, and advocacy		X

Customers expect:

- Choice, convenience, and control[5]
- Reliable, high-quality products and services
- Price-competitive offerings

If customers don't like the way a company treats them or makes them feel, they vote with their mouth (negative word-of-mouth), feet (churn) and fingers (consumer-generated media). This is definitely true of the Generation Y, and increasingly also applies to the Generations BY. Ultimately, through their behavior and their voice, customers decide what, to them, the real value of a company is. It's only by cooperating with customers, working towards common objectives in partnership towards what is perceived as value by both players, that value can be created.

Current developments in the digital world and the abundance of choice consumers have are confusing to many consumers. Translated into a value proposition, this offers a lot of opportunities to create intangible features or, even better, benefits with which companies can differentiate their value proposition from their competitors. Consumers feel everyone offers the same. The challenge is to design a value proposition that can help a brand become a brand experience.

To give you an example, think about the digital home environment. While consumers may be intrigued, the majority are unable or don't want to invest the time and the brainpower to assess how it will affect their home environment.

- What does the convergence of television, telephone and Internet mean for me as a consumer?
- How does the general migration to IP (Internet Protocol) impact me?
- How does it change the way I use the Internet, telephone or television?
- How will it affect the other members of my family?

In addition, many consumers are concerned about the potential dangers, from the concern of parents about their children's safety to financial matters (online banking, mobile phone banking, etc.), as well as the potential abuse of personal details (identity theft).

Companies in this arena have started to create, communicate, and deliver value propositions that are targeted to creating trust that they as a company and their employees are there for customers as trustworthy advisers in the digital world.

"Our Difference: It's about people, not technology. We simplify, advise and guide so that customers can participate in the digital world at their own pace and fit their own needs."

This brand difference was successfully introduced by UPC Broadband in Europe after the 2.5-year transformation process I initiated to ensure that the organization had completely mapped out and was able to deliver the value proposition that matched this brand difference.

Employee Advocacy

Businesses across all industries are becoming people businesses, no matter how technological they may appear to be. It's not the technology that sets companies apart, but the way the people who represent a company interact with customers. People can't help themselves—whatever is inside will leak out. If the employees of your company feel happy in the environment they work, if they love their job and their company, if they feel valued and respected, if they feel autonomy with respect to how they treat customers (be they internal or external), their interactions with customers are bound to create customer advocacy. Employee advocacy creates customer advocacy. Without employee advocacy, creating customer advocacy is a "mission impossible."

Organizational Transformation

Customer advocacy is the ultimate differentiator, the most sustainable one, and the one which is the hardest to copy. It is also probably the hardest challenge many companies face because it requires a transformation. Not process redesign, lean Six Sigma, CRM technology, SAP, or any of the other kind of change agents we've seen in the past. It requires alignment at all levels within a company to create sustainable customer advocacy—not just from a hierarchical perspective, or, for that matter, a process perspective.

STRATEGY

The vision and strategy of a company need to be aligned with creating customer advocacy. Nicely worded vision and values that are not consistent with the strategic agenda of a company (which, sadly, is sometimes hidden from the organization with the exception of top management) will achieve the opposite of employee and customer advocacy. When the strategic goals of a company are solely focused on the short term, increasing shareholder value and everything a company does is driven by this purpose, the company is centered around a sense of purpose that by its nature is incapable of creating a "compelling connective quality."[6] Therefore, it is unable to be meaningful and valuable on a sensory emotional (human being) level to the people who work there or, for that matter, its customers.

STRUCTURE

A company with a hierarchical structure where the powers that rule are based on the position a person occupies and where the people at the top are surrounded by 'yea-sayers' is ruled by the fear of standing out, of making mistakes, and of being punished for it. Ownership and responsibility are managed by controlling risks and objectives, not by creating an environment where people are empowered to take ownership and responsibility themselves. This kind of structure is at its core incapable of creating an environment where people are (en-)able(-d) to create trust, both between the people within the company and the people they interact with outside the company, such as customers. Creating employee and customer advocacy requires high-level organizational design that is first and foremost customer- and people-driven.

GOVERNANCE

Governance relates to the manner in which boards or the like direct a corporation, the laws and customs (rules) applying to that direction, consistent management, cohesive policies, processes and decision-rights for a given area of responsibility.[7] Governance related to creating employee and customer advocacy requires the highest level of "walking the talk" possible, of consistently setting an example through their own behavior and of creating policies, processes and decision/rights that are consistent with the goal of creating employee and customer advocacy. In case you are looking for some inspiration for walking the talk, I can recommend a short movie (www. thewalkthetalkmovie.com) based on a book by Eric Harvey and Steve Ventura.[8]

PERFORMANCE MANAGEMENT

Performance measurement is the process of assessing progress toward achieving predetermined goals. Performance management is building on that process, adding the relevant communication and action on the progress achieved against these predetermined goals.[9] Employee and customer advocacy requires performance management that sets the kind of goals that create employee and customer advocacy and rewards the achievement of these goals.

PROCESSES AND SYSTEMS

The goal of processes and systems for the longest time has been company-centric and output-driven, creating and increasing efficiency. Although efficiency is still important, the days are over when efficiency can still primarily be improved by processes and systems. Hence its decreasing power as a differentiator. Advocacy is outcome- or impact-driven, and creates efficiency and effectiveness from an employee and a customer perspective. With that, the focus for processes and systems has shifted to enabling employees and customers to improve the outcome, the convenience of doing business, and the level of control, and to help customers (and employees) deal with the abundance of choices they have. This then offers a customer the best solution a company has to offer in ways that suit the customer the best with the best conditions and offers employees the tools (processes and systems) that enable them to adequately support the customers they serve and to balance customer and company interests.

CAPABILITIES, BEHAVIOR AND LEADERSHIP

Creating employee and customer advocacy requires transformational leadership[10] that supports the kind of environment where people, independent of formal positions, engage each other and raise one another to higher levels of motivation, commitment, responsibility, quality, and performance. It requires the highest level of "walking the talk" possible, with upper management consistently setting an example through their own behavior. Capabilities, behavior, and leadership need to be consistent with the goal of creating employee and customer advocacy. The people within an organization need to have the right character and competencies and display the right behavior and leadership style to make advocacy happen. In an environment and culture where people feel trusted, valued, and respected as a human being (not as a human doing), they can authentically be the human being they are and will start to take ownership and responsibility for what they do. That's where employee advocacy starts.

How much control companies will have over the advocacy of their employees and customers largely depends on not just a successful transformation of their organization, but ultimately on how successful they will be at consistently creating expectations with their employees and customers and the consistency of their delivery. That's what builds trust. Trust builds loyalty and, ultimately, advocacy. The authenticity of the people representing an organization, from top to bottom, is the most critical success factor for the sustainability of customer advocacy.

Net Promoter Score

Markets circumstances such as commoditization, market saturation, and hyper-competition have turned customer loyalty into a boardroom topic and created a sense of urgency to do something about it. The Net Promoter Score (NPS), the net percentage of customers (promoters) recommending a company to their family and friends, was introduced by Fred Reichheld,[11] a U.S. business author and strategist and widely recognized as one of the world's leading authorities on business loyalty, in 2006. His research, which provided tangible proof of the correlation between the recommendation of customers and the profitable growth potential of companies, received a warm welcome. Many CEOs have added NPS as a key performance indicator (KPI) to the management toolkit of their company. GE, for instance, standardized NPS across all the businesses. To quote their CEO: "It's useful to have at least one score standard across the company, because that way we can spread the learning." Amazon, eBay, and Harley Davidson are other examples of companies using the NPS. Customer advocacy is not just another name for the same concept.

The first time I started measuring the Net Promoter Score was in September 2005. The three years of experience with NPS were an intrinsic part of the vision I developed. The NPS in itself is a valuable KPI, but it's less useful without the knowledge and the tools to manage it. Reichheld focuses primarily on customers and frontline employees without addressing the organization as a whole or measuring the NPS of employees, whereas NPS is equally useful to measure the recommendation rate internally. This realization helped me develop my thinking about how companies can manage the NPS not just of customers but also of employees.

Employee and customer advocacy are the other side of the coin of reputation management, consisting of brand reputation, corporate social responsibility, and risk and crisis management. Corporate social responsibility initiatives set out to portray a brand and a company as socially responsible. Risk and crisis management manages the reputational risks and the impact on the reputation of a brand and a company in times of crises. Employee and customer advocacy addresses the reputation your company has with its two most important stakeholders. The NPS is *the* KPI to measure the output, but doesn't enable you to create employee and customer advocacy, to manage it, to improve it, or to make it sustainable.

Consider traditional customer satisfaction research. Simply knowing what percentage of your customers is (un-)satisfied doesn't supply the information you need to improve that percentage. Likewise, the NPS gives a score, but doesn't tell how to improve that score. The NPS itself doesn't address the complexity of the components that together result in the score. Reichheld touches on this in his book, but working with it as I have over the years has enabled me to develop a more complete and holistic approach from an organizational perspective. Although the NPS is useful and it can be linked with the profitable growth potential, it doesn't tell you how to influence or improve it, which makes it quite a dangerous KPI if looked at it in isolation.

By now, I hope you have started to get an idea about the complexity of the components that together enable an organization to create employee and customer advocacy. It starts with the DNA or the intrinsic profile of all the people (not just the frontline employees) in your company, their value systems (or inner values), their beliefs, the culture, and their dilemmas. You can create alignment in all other areas, such as the ones mentioned above, but in order to be able to transform your organization into one that is successfully and sustainably able to create employee and customer advocacy, you need to address the core. NPS gives you the actual score at a certain point in time. In Chapter 7, "How to make Customer Advocacy Sustainable," I will discuss this more in-depth.

Brand Advocacy
Some marketing literature uses the term "Brand Advocacy." The UK brand agency Promise executes a yearly "Promise Index" that ranks brands according to their promise gap, i.e., the difference between the image consumers have of them and the actual experience. Brand Advocacy is, in my view, a synonym for Customer Advocacy. I champion the term "Customer Advocacy," because it stipulates the source, i.e., the customer.

Conclusion

Markets have become conversations. Consumer generated content, the often international community, and the inner circle now have a larger impact on preferences than any traditional communication channel. The perception of a brand and the emotional connection with a brand is a growing factor in the choice process of a consumer.

The power has shifted to consumers. The way a company makes its customers feel and the value as perceived by a customer increasingly is decisive for the success of a company. Consumers have so much choice that preferences and emotions have become crucial. The tangible attributes of a product have far less influence on consumer preference than subconscious sensory and emotional elements. The domains companies traditionally compete in are changing dramatically and rapidly. These changes erode the traditional competitive power of companies, and undermine their customer relationships. Meanwhile, one of the few means for organic growth companies have left is to grow the share of wallet of their existing customer base. In other words, create a relationship of trust and loyalty with their existing customers.

Customer advocacy is the ultimate differentiator and the most sustainable one. It requires alignment at all levels of a company to create sustainable customer advocacy from the strategy, structure, governance, performance management, processes and systems, down to the capabilities, behavior, and leadership style of the people representing a company. Employee advocacy precedes customer advocacy.

Customer advocacy is the next competitive battleground. The upside is huge direct business development potential. The downside are blogstorms, googlebombing, etc.; PR risks when customers feel they have not been taken seriously.

CHAPTER 3

Our World Is Changing

We have seen how consumer and industry developments force companies to transform their organizations and reconsider their value propositions. Company reputations are a significant part of the equation, both from a customer and an employee perspective, whereas generational differences compel companies to reconsider their role both as a provider and as an employer. The authenticity and ethics a company portrays in the way it interacts more and more becomes a distinguishing factor for employees and customers.

A MULTITUDE OF DEVELOPMENTS is changing the arenas in which companies traditionally compete. These changes erode the traditional competitive power of companies and undermine their employee and customer relationships. In this chapter I will take a closer look at what the most relevant changes are, what causes them, and how they change the playing field in many industries and businesses.

Industry Developments
Industry developments force companies to reconsider their core business and business models. Traditional industries such as telecom, television, banking, insurance, mortgages,

fast-moving consumer goods, fashion—basically every industry one way or another—are affected by increasing complexity. Companies in many industries are confronted with a severe intensification of competition. The big difference is that we have migrated from an era of restriction to an era of choice. The following main trends force companies to reconsider the core of their business and models:

- Consolidation
- Internationalization
- Shifts of traditional roles in the value chain
- The pre-requisite of efficiency
- Convergence
- New market entrants
- Commoditization
- Market saturation

While these trends erode the traditional competitive strength and undermine customer relationships, companies are becoming increasingly dependent on the existing relationships with and loyalty of their customers for the sustainability, the profitability, and the organic growth of their business. The challenge for most companies in the years to come will be to improve the quality of their intangible assets—their employees and their customers—to improve the quality of the relationships with their employees and their customers and to see it all translate into employee and customer advocacy as the most effective (and efficient) means to generate profitable growth. It cannot be a coincidence that Gary Hamel's latest book *The Future of Management*[12] deals with the topic of Management Innovation—"new ways of mobilizing talent, allocating resources, and building strategies."

CONSOLIDATION

Mergers and acquisitions nowadays are more often driven by a desire to generate growth than to create synergies and economies of scale or to decrease the number of players in national and local markets. The remaining players increase their size and market power. This trend may seem to contradict what I said about the abundance of choice consumers have, but actually it both decreases and increases choices. Though companies can integrate existing players in their markets, they also face competition from other players, often with deep pockets (money to invest, for instance, in marketing) who cross the borders and enter their domains through acquisitions.

INTERNATIONALIZATION

This trend has several sides. Companies become multinational players as a result of consolidation and the World Wide Web. Companies that traditionally held a strong position on a national scale see themselves faced with strong international competitors. New players enter the marketplace, intensifying the competition and the fight for revenue (and organic growth). An example is ING Direct (an Internet bank, initiated and owned by ING, a large player in the Dutch market) launched in 2001 in Canada and soon after in the U.S. In a market with almost 10,000 banks already, they successfully started an online bank, offering a simple and attractive way to save money for the common American and growing their business largely through customer advocacy. In 2008, they are one of the ten largest banks in the U.S. Measured in deposits, they rank seventeenth. Meanwhile, they also successfully started to offer mortgages and online brokerage.

The Internet has also opened up possibilities for different kinds of players. The Web has made it possible for small players to address a global market. It has also made it possible for players, both more traditional or new entrants, to sell quantities that were not economically feasible in the mass market dynamics to a global audience (known as 'the long tail'[13]).

SHIFTS OF TRADITIONAL ROLES IN THE VALUE CHAIN

Traditional roles in value chains are changing, impacting business structures and business models. The Internet has made it possible for companies in many industries to eliminate traditional roles in their value chain, such as wholesale trade and shops, and to address consumers directly.

The most profound example is the entertainment industry, where consumers used to be required to buy a CD or a DVD to enjoy music or a movie. Nowadays you can download content directly from the artist or through companies that used to sell only hardware and software (such as Apple's iTunes and AppleTV) on a server at home, without any involvement of a physical device. The implications for traditional parties in the value chain, such as record companies, stores that sell CDs and DVDs, or stores that rent DVDs, has been a decrease in business such that some were even forced to go out of business.

With the introduction of e-books, we see the same phenomenon happening to books. Instead of buying the physical book, people download the content and read the book on a digital device, which means that traditional bookstores will see a decrease in the number of books they sell.

Real estate agents are losing business to online consumer communities where people put their houses up for sale without the involvement of professionals.

Headhunters and recruitment agencies are losing business through online social communities such as

LinkedIn, Plaxo, Xing, etc., where supply and demand find each other directly without their involvement.

Insurance companies have ruled out their intermediaries because the Web has made it much easier to communicate with consumers directly.

Delivery companies are fighting the decrease of the amount of mail due to the fact that consumers prefer to communicate through email instead of snail mail (and of course the increasing amount of competition due to the privatization of this industry). On the other hand, they benefit from the increase of online shopping, due to the increase in the quantity of products consumers buy online and get delivered straight to their homes. Online shopping enables producers to communicate with and sell directly to consumers, excluding traditional roles, such as wholesale trade and shops, in the value chain.

EFFICIENCY HAS BECOME A PRE-REQUISITE

Total quality management, ISO, Kai Zen, (Lean) Six Sigma, Business Process Redesign, to name but a few, are approaches we've seen in the last decades to optimize efficiency. They have surpassed their differentiating power. Efficiency has to be good to be a player at all. If a company hasn't created its own learning curve by now and isn't completely savvy in those arenas today, it's too late. Today efficiency is the starting point. It's the added value that companies offer on top of that that allows a sustainable competitive advantage.

CONVERGENCE

Convergence is taking place at different levels.

First, we have the convergence of media, especially now that everything is moving to IP. Mobile phones have only been around for the masses for around ten years. Now our mobile phone is a phone, an organizer, an address book, a camera (sometimes even video), an entertainment device for music and video (TV), and a GPS for personal navigation. Watching TV is also an experience that is changing rapidly. Gone are the days that you are forced to watch what the broadcasting companies broadcast. You now can watch what you want, when and where you want it. You can watch previously downloaded content from a server that is part of your home environment. You can integrate your TV screen with your mail system and your voice system, so that while you're watching TV you can see messages or calls coming in and decide then and there to stop what you are watching to answer the call or the message. After you are finished, you can resume the program you were watching from where you stopped it. These examples show that there is not only convergence of media, but also of function.

Second, there is a different kind of convergence taking place—the kind that forces companies to rethink the way they are organized. In a world where markets have become conversations and the voice of the customer starts to play a bigger role than the voice companies manage themselves (marketing communications, PR), the traditional "silo" organizational model has started to become ineffective. Can marketing exist disconnected from the departments that are responsible for the delivery to the customer, such as sales and service? Can innovation and product development exist in an isolated lab environment? Can IT exist isolated from the business? The way customers have started to manifest themselves forces companies to rethink the way they are organized and to take into consideration ultimately what role each silo plays in a mutual end goal: delivering value to all stakeholders, but first and foremost to customers.

NEW MARKET ENTRANTS

New market entrants often have the advantage not having to make the kind of investment traditional players had to make when building or entering those markets.

Telecom companies have suffered large losses of customers to Voice-over IP (VoIP) providers, who were able to enter this market without having to invest in infrastructure because they use the existing infrastructure traditional players like telecom and cable companies built. Traditional players are losing their customers to players like Skype and Vonage, who use the traditional infrastructure, and there's nothing traditionals can do about it.

The same stands to happen and is to a certain degree already happening with the replacement of traditional TV by IPTV. Apple just re-launched their AppleTV, Joost.com is beta-testing (owned by the founders and former owners of Skype). These companies offer digital TV through the Web, luring customers away from traditional players like cable companies. They use the existing infrastructure. The largest threat for traditional players, like telecom and cable companies, is that they become to consumers merely a "dumb pipe". In other words, you, as a consumer, only see them as a dumb pipe that connects you to the Web. You buy all the products and services from online providers.

Once started as a search engine, Google is becoming more and more of a threat for traditional players for advertising. Traditional media such as newspapers and television are being forced to reconsider their business models.

eBay has taken away a lot of turnover from traditional players in markets by making the selling of second-hand goods easy and attractive for consumers. Think for instance about baby gear, like car seats and strollers.

Among new parents, it is almost politically incorrect to buy these new nowadays.

eBay has grown its business based on cross-references from consumers and sellers within their online community. They have successfully used that community to expand their services to banking. What started as a natural way of making payments between sellers and buyers easier (often micro and border crossing) has successfully been turned into PayPal, an online bank that within Europe alone has around 35 million customers. Since July 2007 PayPal holds a banking license for Europe. With that, PayPal is positioned to become a serious competitor for traditional banks within Europe. Other players like www.mint.com and www.wesabe.com have entered the personal financial services domain with innovative value propositions.

COMMODITIZATION

Many markets (telecom, cable, content, and also computer equipment, entertainment equipment, home supplies, hardware, cars, fashion—I could go on) have become saturated, and products and services of different producers and providers are interchangeable. Traditional ways for companies to differentiate themselves have become problematic. Price, quality, accessibility, delivery, product features and many other facets have all been squeezed, redeveloped, improved, and modified. These are now very limited in their ability to serve as differentiators.

Before deciding to buy, consumers browse the Web for information on the quality of products and prices, they check Weblogs to find out what other consumers say about a product and different brands, they ask around, and finally, they decide to buy. What and where they buy has become more a matter of what the experiences of other consumers have been with a product and a brand than what the producer and the brand say about themselves.

Price does play a role and there will always be a segment of consumers who go primarily for the lowest price, but the quantity of consumers for whom the total package is decisive is much larger and growing. For those consumers, the total package is the sum of everything that constitutes the value proposition a company has to offer. Therefore, that value proposition has to be clear to consumers. Companies are not used to thinking along those lines. They think that the product or the service is the value proposition. But that's the part consumers take for granted, or better, assume to be right. It's the combination of tangible features and intangible benefits that make a consumer take their business to a specific company. Service components (intangible attributes) include: "How will a company help me make the right choice?" in the abundance of choices; "How will a company support me after I've bought from them?"; "How do I feel as a result of every interaction with people representing a company?"; "How will they help me to make sure that the choice I've made continues to be the right choice for me when circumstances change?"; "Do they listen to me?"; "Do they show me that they authentically care?"

MARKET SATURATION

As I said, many markets are saturated and consumers have more choice than ever for anything and everything, from their daily groceries to more durable products. Quality and price are basics and consumers base their decisions increasingly on emotional value rather than functional (rational) value, which they almost take for granted.

Think of the concept of Lovemarks, introduced by Kevin Roberts in 2005[14]. He claims, "Brands have run out

WHEN YOU CARE, PEOPLE NOTICE

of juice. More and more people in the world have grown to expect great performance from products, services and experiences. Lovemarks transcend brands. They deliver beyond your expectations of great performance. Like great brands, they sit on top of high levels of respect—but there the similarities end. Lovemarks reach your heart as well as your mind, creating an intimate, emotional connection that you just can't live without. Ever. Take a brand away and people will find a replacement. Take a Lovemark away and people will protest its absence. Lovemarks are a relationship, not a mere transaction. You don't just buy Lovemarks, you embrace them passionately. That's why you never want to let go. Put simply, Lovemarks inspire Loyalty Beyond Reason."[15]

Reputational Developments

Customers are becoming more vocal every day. Consumer-generated media (CGM) is the fastest-growing media. The voice of the customer is getting stronger and heard by more other consumers, and recommendation is becoming more powerful. What consumers create and share with each other is more often than not inspired by relevant customer experiences. Companies get trashed in CGM such as blogs, message boards and forums, review/rating sites, and video-logs, and brand reputations get branded and trashed by negative recommendations, chasing away (potential) customers.

Many companies suffer from a branded reputation. Their behavior, sometimes in the past, sometimes still today, has delivered a reputation in the marketplace that disqualifies any marketing or PR message they put out themselves. Often their behavior was or is caused by putting short-term goals as directed by their shareholders first. Companies can no longer be successful with this business model, because consumers have so much choice and the power has shifted to them.

As I have experienced at UPC Broadband, it is possible to turn the situation around. Especially in such a saturated market as the TV, broadband and telephony market, customers are fed up with suppliers who disregard them. They respond positively to a company that really changes its behavior. When I started at UPC Broadband in the beginning of 2004, the company was *the* example of bad customer service and experiences in some of its countries. By 2007 the company ranked as the most customer friendly provider of TV, broadband and telephony, in an industry with a bad reputation altogether. I started to measure the advocacy of its customers at the end of 2005. Since then, the NPS[16] increased in some cases thirty percent. If you are serious about it, you can change the reputation of a brand. It does take a lot of time and stamina, though, to prepare an organization for such a shift. A good reputation is also very vulnerable. It requires consistency in the delivery of the customer experience, day after day, with every interaction, because customers are even more relentless when a company returns to its old behavior.

When a company suffers from a branded reputation, the people who work for that organization or the people it is trying to recruit are also impacted, which adds to the complexity. A branded reputation has an impact on companies' recruitment potential, which is a matter of growing concern as labor markets are getting tighter. It also has an impact on employees working for a company. Employees who cannot be proud of their company cannot be ambassadors for that company. Whatever is inside, will leak out.

Internal Developments
Careers used to be built on how successful people were in dealing with the unwritten rules of company politics. Authority used to be linked to the position a person held in the hierarchy, and coalitions and alliances were formed

based on hierarchic positions. If your company still works this way, it will be a giant leap to transform it into an organization that is capable of creating employee and customer advocacy. Creating employee and customer advocacy requires authenticity. Authenticity requires other skills, such as honesty, integrity, and ethics initially driven by the inner values and the value systems at a personal level. Now that consumers judge and critique companies on their authenticity, they look for the inner values not of a company but of the people representing a company, from the top all the way to the people who deal directly with the customer. When you care, people notice.

As Stephen Covey describes it in his book *The Speed of Trust* (2006),[17] "(S x E) T = R. Strategy times Execution, multiplied by Trust equals Results." The lower the level of trust, the less the values are shared and the identity is consistent, the higher the level of politics and unwritten rules within that company. The more political the environment, the more individual the values and the goals. Low trust slows down the speed, increases the cost, and decreases the results, whereas high trust increases the speed, decreases the cost, and increases the results. Nowadays mobilizing and managing talent is not about control, but about creating environments where people feel respected and valued, and are (en-)able(-d) to contribute from who they are as a human being, not as a human doing.

What customers want with respect to the people who represent a company:

- A real person to interact with when they want;
- A reliable and trustworthy person who gives them the feeling he really cares, not just about them but about everything, including their job and the company they represent (whether it's a company representative

giving an interview on national TV or a Customer Service Representative);

- A real person who listens, shows empathy and compassion, and authentically shows they care about the customer as a person. Being nice and polite is not enough;
- A person who has the mandate to solve their problem and doesn't hide behind internal policies, procedures or systems;
- A person who is a trusted source of information and an advisor who can look at the world from the perspective of the customer and is capable of creating balance between the interests of the individual customer and the company they represent.

Activating customer advocacy as a source of sustainable competitive advantage requires authenticity, honesty, integrity, ethics, and inner values of the people who represent a company to appeal to the people (customers) a company is attempting to attract.

The way a company's employees interact with customers sets a company apart.

The people on the forefront of a company, who interface with customers on a daily basis, especially need enough space, trust and self-respect to be able to interface with customers on a personal level.

EMPLOYEES: GENERATION Y

As mentioned earlier, the age group born after 1980 bases its employment decisions on how authentic a company is. These millennials, Generation Y, or the gaming generation decides, for example, to play a game because of the ethics displayed.

The Financial Times reported in an article in September 2006 about the gaming generation as a workforce[18]. Born into the information age, they are very capable in processing the avalanche of information that comes to them every day. The way they learn, work, and pursue careers is developed in the gaming environment they inhabit. The working morale of the "gaming man": "[They base] work on completed tasks, rather than other measures of work effort. ... These kids quit when they are frustrated trying to finish a quest that will get them to the next level. ... They are the future. And they're coming soon to a workplace near you." In other words, don't even think of trying to manage this generation on a task level, because this generation bases its work satisfaction on "completed tasks"; they "quit when they are frustrated trying to finish a quest that will get them to the next level," so without visibility of, and clear levels (the set of tasks leading up to the goal they need to achieve) they will not play.

In February 2008 the U.S. Website Monsterboard[19] presented a questionnaire to its visitors, asking them to choose between three options about what they are looking for in a job:

1. Job security.
2. Financial gain and advancement.
3. Challenging work that is fulfilling, the rest will follow.

The votes were divided as follows:

1. 20%
2. 26%
3. 53%

"Challenging work that is fulfilling, the rest will follow" got the majority of the votes. Generation Y represents a large part of the visitors of Monsterboard.

Granted, they are not the only workforce you need to take into consideration, especially not as the call for later retirement gets louder. The question is, what do you need to do to attract and keep this generation as a workforce? Is it possible to offer this generation the workplace requirements they are seeking?

EMPLOYEES: GENERATIONS BY

Generations BY are the generations born before Generation Y. The industrial age is characterized by corporate ecosystems,[20] "a company-centric, efficiency-driven view of value creation that has shaped our industrial infrastructure and the entire business system." Or, as Gary Hamel describes it in his latest book "The Future of Management" on management innovation: "...efficiency-centric, bureaucracy-based managerial paradigm."[21] Though the industrial age was followed by the information age, a lot of the paradigms inherited from the industrial age still apply. Meanwhile, knowledge and information no longer represent power, because knowledge and information too have become commodities. We have entered into the Transformational Age.[22] The focus has shifted to real-time customer ecosystems, [23] "where the ultimate control and determination of value lies with the customer, and is based on both functional (rational) value and emotional value." The industrial age paradigms don't apply in the transformational age.

Under the industrial age paradigms, employees are managed in alignment with the corporate ecosystem, in a company-centric, efficiency-driven way. Control is at the core of management. Employees are treated as human resources, managed at a task level. The lower the level, the more robotized (controlled) the tasks and activities. Employees are trained to execute steps in processes, without an overview, understanding of, or influence on the process as a whole, nor the confidence to take ownership.

Many companies migrate the simple customer interactions to self-service online environments, where customers are more than happy to do it themselves, when and where it suits them. This leaves the more complicated interactions in the hands of robotized employees, not fit for the demands for which customers specifically seek interactions with them. Think of online banking. One of the largest consumer banks in the Netherlands (a country with a population of 16 million people) used to have about 400 million visits a year from customers to their branch offices in the days before online banking. Nowadays the average is about 4 million customer visits per year. You can imagine that when a customer does visit a branch office nowadays, he requires quality time, attention, and advice. This has huge implications for what kind of people need to serve him.

For the Generation Y, work is an intrinsic part of their way of life. For the Generations BY, work is becoming part of their way of life as well. Hence the number of people who quit their corporate jobs to become self employed to balance their personal and business life. Employees who lack a degree of wellbeing in their work/life balance cannot contribute to the full extent of their abilities. The quality of their performance is impacted by their sense of wellbeing in their work environment. Some people from the Generations BY may endure this in their work life with repercussions for the efficiency and the results they are able to achieve. Those who can't more often than not suffer burn-out, or after a sabbatical take a breather from their work life and make a dramatic shift, choosing completely different ways to make a living. These events come at a high cost for companies, costs that further erode already decreasing margins. Generation Y will not even consider working in such an environment.

The role of employees, especially those who have interactions with customers at the core of their daily work, is changing. In many businesses and industries, they need to become trusted advisors and guides for customers. They especially are the ones against whom customers evaluate a brand and a company. Customers evaluate them and the company they represent based on the authenticity, ethics, and values they portray in their interactions.

It is against this background that companies can no longer afford to deal with employees in ways that were feasible under the industrial-age paradigms. In an environment where people notice when you care, the way a company makes employees feel becomes key to the success of a company. Whatever is inside will leak out. When employees don't feel cared for, valued, respected or recognized, how can they possibly give customers those feelings?

Empowerment has often been abused to give employees an alleged sense of being valued and respected, to give them a sense that they are operating from their own inner values. But in most cases what this meant was that the value system of the controllable machine was forced on them, reinforcing their human doing, instead of creating room for them as a human being.

In the vast library of books on management, a definition of this often abused word empowerment comes from Manfred Kets de Vries[24] in his small treasure of a book called *The Happiness Equation*[25] first published in 2000: "I encourage executives to create what I call 'authentizotic organizations.' Authenticity implies that an organization has a compelling connective quality for its employees in its vision, mission, culture and structure. In other words, it creates meaning for the people who work there. ... Zoteekos ('vital to life') applies to organizations that allow for self-assertion in the workplace and produce a sense of effectiveness and competency, autonomy, initiative, creativity, entrepreneurship, and organizations in which people feel generally happy."

Kets de Vries talks about the people who work for an organization and addresses what the environment of an organization does for its employees as a human being. That's where he really hits the core. The environment he describes in his definition really communicates respect, a sense of employees as human beings.

The urgency is growing to consider the actual reason for being of employees. Companies need to profile the values, ethics, culture, and behaviors of the people in their organization against their business objectives (their strategy), and their customers or customer segments (Chapter 7, Customer Advocacy Indicator). If employee and customer advocacy is part of your business objective, you need to start with making sure that the inner values, ethics, culture, and behaviors of all the people from top to bottom within your organization are adequate to do the job.

Accessing the "hidden asset"[26] of a company and unveiling the growth potential in today's business dynamics requires:

- Managers and every employee to become leaders;
- Leaders to engage with others from who they are as a person, in such a way that the people within the organization, independent of formal positions, raise one another to higher levels of motivation, commitment, responsibility, quality, and performance, and stop letting their ego rule who they are;
- Leaders who create an environment in which people can be people;
- Employees who feel confident in every respect about interacting with customers as people.

Creating employee and customer advocacy requires a shift in leadership style from managing from industrial paradigms focused on control to leadership based on setting an example, creating a strong sense of purpose, creating a compelling connective quality, trust, respect, recognition, autonomy, and creating a safe environment for the people in an organization. It requires people who are willing and capable to attack company politics head on, to transform an organization into a high-trust environment. It requires people who are capable of setting an example, who show integrity, who are open about their own intent, about their own truth, and about their own values. That takes a lot of courage and will not always be easy.

Creating employee and customer advocacy requires companies to invest in the personal development of all the people in their company. It requires companies to turn their employees into ambassadors for their organization, taking ownership and responsibility for their personal contributions, and being proud of their company. Only when employees are advocates for the organization will they be able to build relationships based on trust with the customers they serve and turn those customers into advocates. In a world where markets have become conversations and the customer is, quite literally, at the forefront of business, that is the ultimate differentiator. Customer advocacy is authentic and essentially selfless behavior of customers. You can't pay them a premium to become an advocate. It requires authentic behavior from a company and its employees. Similarly, you can't pay employees a premium or a bonus to become an ambassador. It's something they authentically need to feel inside.

"In 2005, Towers Perrin, a consulting company, executed a survey among 86.000 employees working for large and medium-sized companies in 16 countries.[27] ... According to the study, a mere 14% of employees around the world are highly engaged in their work, while 24% are disengaged. Everyone else is somewhere in the tepid middle. In other words, roughly 85% of those at work around the world ... are giving less of themselves than they could."

This research shows on the one hand the size of the challenge and on the other gives you a clue about the potential of the hidden asset your employees represent. What if you can turn around 85% of your employees giving less of themselves than they could to 85% giving more of themselves than you could have predicted?

INTERNAL NETWORKS

As mentioned earlier, the way consumers have started to manifest themselves forces companies to rethink the way they are organized and the way they innovate, and to take into consideration how each corporate silo affects the mutual end goal, which has become delivering value to all its stakeholders but first and foremost to its employees and customers. Creating customer advocacy requires companies to create a flawless and consistent experience across the board, throughout the customer activity cycle, from brand and marketing messages, to the actual usage of a product or service, the way they innovate, and any interaction with people representing a company.

Corporate ecosystems, with their company-centric, efficiency-driven view of value creation, are more often than not managed to create value for shareholders, not employees or customers. Hierarchical structures don't empower employees to take ownership and responsibility, but encourage them to hide behind the structure and finger-point instead. Some companies try to address this challenge by adding a chief customer officer or a chief advocacy officer. The question is if that is an adequate solution. On the one hand it may be a useful way to initiate the required organizational transformation. But as soon as the C-suite representative has to fight for his own position instead of employees and customers, it becomes ineffective. The creation of employee and customer advocacy is everybody's job. It will never work if it's turned into the job of one person or department. If the C-suite representative is the only one who cares, neither employees nor customers will notice.

The success of customer ecosystems, where the ultimate control and determination of value lies with the customer based on functional (rational) and emotional value, requires companies to closely look at the DNA of their organization: from the vision, strategy, short- and long-term goals, how they are organized, how processes are organized, IT systems, governance, and performance management to the inner values, ethics, culture, and behavior of the people representing the organization.

Paradigm shifts are nice, but the key question is how to make them happen. Can people make change happen in other people and make it stick? Many people have tried to make the person of their dreams, the one they think they want to grow old with, change by simply reinforcing desired behavior. "Oh, he or she will change once we're together long and often enough." But what if the other doesn't understand or share your vision of where you want to go in life? On average one in three marriages ends in a divorce. In business, 90% of the mergers fail because "we couldn't change the culture successfully." So, you have to ask yourself, how you can make such a transformation happen?

An organization that can be open about its weaknesses can adequately address those weaknesses. But to be able to do so, companies need courage. They need the courage to look at their DNA. And, in order to make it stick, they need the courage to really change their DNA.

As a metaphor I would like to use the example of a square in a mid-size Dutch town.[28] The municipality had the courage to look at the DNA of this square. The DNA, or value system, of the square was that people needed traffic lights and speed and road signs to control their behavior. To make it more peaceful, they could have just taken out the traffic lights and speed and road signs. But that would not have changed the value system of the square, i.e., the value system people automatically revert to on a town square. It still would have looked like a town square and people would still behave the same way they usually do on town squares. By changing the environment as well, changing the pavement, adding green spaces and water fountains, making it look like a village square, people changed gears to the value system they deploy when crossing a square in a small village. You don't speed through a village square; in a village you behave differently than in a town. Whereas a lot of accidents used to happen in the past and it took a long time to cross the square, no accidents have happened after this make-over, and it takes only seconds to cross the square, whether by car, by bike or on foot.

The way people feel is influenced by their perception of their environment. The way people feel has a major impact on the way they behave. In other words, if you want to make change happen and make it stick, you need to change the way people behave. In order to do that, you need to change the environment and the way people perceive that environment in a way that it changes how people feel so that what people believe in, their inner values, can become the value system that guides them.

Conclusion

A combination of industrial developments is eroding the traditional competitive strength of companies and undermining employee and customer relationships. In the reputation economy, companies suffer the consequences from their branded reputations.

What customers want with respect to the people who represent a company:

- Choice, convenience, and control;
- Reliable, high quality products and services;
- Price-competitive offerings;
- To feel good about themselves when interacting with a company, and as a result of interacting with a company.

The challenges and the opportunities for companies are:

- To offer customers what they want, to create a value proposition that offers not just the tangible features but also the intangible benefits that feed the subconscious sensory and emotional elements with which companies can differentiate themselves from their competitors and that can help a brand become an experience.
- As labor markets get tighter, the make-up of companies makes it even harder for them to not only recruit people, but also to keep their employees and harvest their true potential. Generation Y rejects companies as a potential employer based on the ethics and authenticity of a company. Generations BY choose completely different ways to make a living, often opting for self employment.
- Industrial-age paradigms and ways of working are becoming a disqualifier for success in an age where people, be it employees or customers, are assessing companies on their ability to create an environment and experiences that are meaningful for them as human beings.

- To create customer advocacy, companies need to reconsider the role of their employees. Employees are a capital-generating asset. Employees need a high-trust and meaningful environment to be able to create high trust and meaningful experiences for customers. The personal growth and self-confidence of employees needs to be enabled, so they can connect with customers on a personal level. Employees who operate as part of a high-trust environment, will contribute largely to creating a high-trust relationship with customers. Employees are a key differentiator in a crowded marketplace, a key source of sustainable competitive advantage, and a key source of creating value for customers, and as such represent an important component of the brand. Customer-facing employees are inspiring and trusted guides and advisors for customers. Customer-facing employees contribute materially to customer retention, customer loyalty, and the creation of customer advocacy. Customer-facing employees are often the largest and cheapest sales channel, making the best quality sales, increasing the share of wallet through cross- and up-selling, and harvesting on the growth potential of the existing customer base, all while operating more efficiently than ever before. Building stakeholder trust starts with your employees (employee advocacy).

Leadership

*Creating customer advocacy requires a shift in the leadership
style of the people in companies; from managing from the
industrial paradigms focused on control,[29] to leadership
based on setting an example, creating a strong sense of
purpose, creating a "compelling connective quality," meaning,
trust, respect, recognition, autonomy, and creating a safe
environment for the people in an organization. All of this
starts with self-confidence.*

MANY RELEVANT AND well documented books have
been published and are being published every
day about leadership. I don't intend to add to
that vast amount of books with this chapter. The reason
you do find a chapter in this book with this title is that
I want to share with you the leadership framework I
developed while transforming companies into being able
to create employee and customer advocacy. Leadership as
I see it is not limited to the higher levels in an organization,
but each and every person is a leader no matter what their
level or the authority of their position. This framework
is inspired by the "six conditions for leadership" [30] from
Wessel Ganzevoort:

- *Strong Sense of Purpose*
- *Focus on Values*

- *Autonomy*
- *Feedback*
- *Respect and Recognition*
- *A Safe Environment*

On many occasions I've used and tested these six conditions with international audiences and international management development programs, but also with boards of directors when asked to support them in their organizational transformation. The questions I have asked people surrounding these conditions turned out to be so challenging that the participants themselves were often most surprised by their own and each others' answers. I will share the kind of questions I asked in the hopes that you as a reader will be equally surprised by your own answers, and that they will help you understand where you stand personally, where your co-workers stand, and what you and they are prepared and able to do to make a transformation successful.

Strong Sense of Purpose

A successful transformation to becoming a company that is able to create employee and customer advocacy starts with what is driving the people—their shared sense of purpose. To get a feeling for what people want to achieve from an emotional perspective and the degree of alignment between the group of people who set out to make a transformation happen to start creating employee and customer advocacy, I ask them to describe the "emotional endframe"[31] of their employees and customers.

- What is your dream for your employees? How do you want them to feel about themselves and about your company after you have concluded this transformational process? Have you asked your employees what their dream is?

To give you an idea, my personal goal would be that employees are so proud of their company that they are eager to tell anyone who wants to hear it how they love working for that company and how happy they are to be a part of it. When asking employees about their dream, the answers may vary, but interestingly enough, you'll often find that their dream shows a lot of consistency with respect to the dreams of your customers, especially when asking people with customer-facing jobs.

• What is your dream for your customers? How do you want them to feel about themselves and about your company as a result of any and every interaction with your company? Have you asked your customers what their dream is?

My personal goal is that customers are also eager to tell anyone who wants to hear it how they love doing business with that company and why they love it.

• What is your dream for you personally and for your team?

It's obvious that to be able to formulate these dreams, you need to know what it is that would make employees and customers want to tell it to the world.

The next question:

• Is this a shared dream? Is the dream the same among the whole group, or does each member have his or her own individual dream (goal)?

The answers to these question will give you a strong sense of the level of engagement with, commitment to, and alignment for the transformation.

For a transformation to be successful, it needs to be one dream shared by all members of the group that sets out to make it happen. That way, it can become a positive self-fulfilling prophecy. Even when the top-down buy-in isn't explicit from the start, it is possible—though it takes a lot more time—to create an army of ambassadors within and outside a company. However, at some point in the process, top-down and bottom-up have to meet, because when they don't, the sustainability will be endangered.

It doesn't create much of a strong sense of purpose if the employee is merely a tool for the company to increase the wealth of a small group of shareholders. This won't stimulate employees to talk about their employer and their personal contribution with pride every chance they get.

The same goes for customers. How would you feel if you perceived that all you were to a company was a tool to increase its wealth? Would you recommend that company to your friends and family? Or would hold your tongue in silence, feeling embarrassed that you are a customer of that company at all?

Paul de Bloth,[32] professor of Business Spirituality at Nijenrode University (The Netherlands), has designed a business format with three levels:

- Realism (doing);
- Interaction (communication);
- Idealism (vision).

His research concluded that 10% of businesses go bankrupt due to a lack of realism, 30% due to a lack of interaction, and 60% (!) due to a lack of idealism (vision).

A strong sense of purpose creates a strong connection among all stakeholders, especially employees and customers. It's what Kets de Vries calls a "compelling connective quality." This "creates meaning for them, ... applies to organizations that allow for self-assertion in the workplace and produces a sense of effectiveness and competency, autonomy, initiative, creativity, entrepreneurship, and organizations in which people feel generally happy."

A strong sense of purpose starts with respect for customers and employees. It's about connecting the results a company aims to achieve to what is meaningful to customers and employees. So, ask yourself, sincerely, what is meaningful to your customers and your employees? Surely not the fact that your shareholders acquire wealth. That can be a result, but can it be the reason for being of a company? Once a company has identified what is meaningful to its customers and employees, you have the start of what can become a strong sense of purpose.

Focus on Values
Once you have identified the strong sense of purpose, it's time to ask what the values are that support it. You will need those values to identify what persons would perceive it as a "compelling connective quality.". You can use that information to make change happen, because the people within an organization with the right character (the inner values that make the environment meaningful to them as a human being; Chapter 7, Customer Advocacy Indicator) and the right competencies will be your change agents—the people to make change happen. It can be as easy as identifying them in every layer and every corner of a company and turning them into role models. It also helps to start recruiting the right people to make the transformation stick.

The first question:

- What are the values that the people initiating the transformation will use as guiding principles for themselves, each other, and the people around them?

Not those widely communicated corporate values many people can recite, but often haven't internalized. This is about a way of life and walking the talk. So what's the way of life, what's the 'talk' that comes with it, and is everybody authentically engaged and equally committed to walk it? Especially in situations where these don't comply with unwritten rules of company politics, are you willing to attack company politics head on?

• Are you willing to set an example, show integrity, and be open about your intent, truth, and values? Are you willing to create a safe environment, operate from a shared set of values, create a shared and strong sense of purpose, and encourage others to do the same?

Creating employee and customer advocacy requires authenticity. Authenticity requires honesty, integrity, and ethics, starting with and driven by inner values and value systems, and being grounded as human beings through those values. That way, TEAM can truly become "Together Everyone Achieves More." This can unite people in a strong sense of purpose.

Connecting the values that support the strong sense of purpose of a company is exactly where it went wrong when McDonalds introduced "We love to see you smile," according to Larry Light, their chief marketing officer, who subsequently transitioned them to "I'm loving it." At that point, they reached out to their 1.6 million employees worldwide and invested a year to create an environment in which "I'm loving it" could become meaningful to the people who work for McDonalds, before doing anything else. When McDonalds introduced, "We love to see you smile," they had forgotten all about giving their employees a reason to smile. When loving to see people smile is not connected with a value system that gives people, be it customers or employees, a reason to smile, it backfires.

Autonomy
Autonomy is, especially for people who are used to industrial-age paradigms (managing by control) a scary concept. It's suspected to be a threat to efficiency. Middle management is often reluctant because in their perception it takes away the control systems they are using to manage the performance of their teams.

The expression I use here is, "freedom in a framework." Autonomy requires a shared strong sense of purpose, a shared set of values among the people in your organization, and people who are empowered to be self-managing. The strong sense of purpose and the values need to be understandable for everyone, and people need to be able to relate to them. That's what creates the framework. For example, let's look at a garden. It needs to be clear that it is a garden and what the boundaries of the garden are in order for the flowers to be self-managing. People are given the space to bloom in the garden from "the seeds they have within them", from who they are as human beings, without ordering them that they need to be a flower, which flower, which color. In addition, the garden (the environment) needs to intrinsically appeal to people. Therefore the purpose, the values, and the boundaries cannot be hard to understand in order to be felt, energized, and be energizing to people. Think of the example earlier of the town square. The way the environment was adapted affected the way people felt and made them tap into a different value system they already had within them (what Covey would call "character"[33]). People automatically switched from the value system they use when crossing a busy town square to the one they use when crossing a village square. The boundaries were an intrinsic part of the system.

- Are you willing to create an environment where there is space for the transformation to happen?

Changing the concept from a controllable machine to an environment that is meaningful for employees and customers will require people to alter behaviors and attitudes they may have had for a long time. It requires them to take risk, to learn, and to test the boundaries. Therefore I recommend starting with small pilots, preferably in those parts of the organization where it appears to be hard to change. A pilot is less threatening than changing the whole of the organization. It's a way of building a string of little successes, a way of creating champions who can become role models for others. Success is sexy. In other words, it helps you make the new way of life and way to serve spread like a virus, because other people in the organization will want to become part of it. It allows you to give people in all layers of the organization a chance to add to that success from their own creativity, because the risks are lower.

At the basis of autonomy is trust. The lower the trust, the more need there is for control, and vice versa. Trust is a two-way street. To build trust, you need to demonstrate it. If you want your employees to be able to build trust with customers, you need to create an environment in which employees feel trusted.

A sense of purpose can only become strong enough when people are able to let go of control. From managing via industrial paradigms focused on control to leadership that is based on setting an example and creating a strong sense of purpose, a compelling connective quality with trust, respect, recognition, autonomy, distributing accountability, and a safe environment. If you can step up from managing people on a task level to becoming a leader who inspires people and creates the space that makes people take responsibility, and demonstrates trust, results will be the reward for all stakeholders involved.

Autonomy doesn't mean letting go of all controls. It does mean adding a new set of performance indicators, a different way of sharing them, and a different way of sharing accountability. The performance indicators to add are those that create accountability for employees and customers. Link those to the existing performance indicators, which are usually focused on financial and operational performance, and people start to understand how what they do relates to and impacts the bigger picture. It also helps to show people in the organization that you walk the talk—you live the values you say you live. When you say, "Employee and customer advocacy are going to be important performance indicators," share the results with people, share the accountability with them, and link it to their performance indicators such as retention, cross- and up-selling, share of wallet, operational efficiency and even the share price. Gradually, as the employee and customer advocacy start to build, the more traditional performance indicators will start to show a positive trend as well. By sharing this kind of information with people throughout the organization, making people at all levels accountable, and by rewarding them appropriately (instead of just top management), people will start to understand the bigger picture, and when they understand, they will start to work even harder at improving them.

So you see, to let go of control doesn't endanger the efficiency or the results of a company. On the contrary, it creates an environment in which people feel responsible for both, and actively take responsibility and ownership for their role instead of being paralyzed by fear. Remember when you were a child, when someone told you something was your responsibility. When you knew you would be punished for it when something went wrong, you would try to either hide it or put the blame on someone else. If, however, you knew that you would be greeted with open, honest, and respectful feedback and ways to learn from the experience and do better next time, you wouldn't try to hide it or try to put the blame on someone else.

Feedback

Giving feedback in an open and honest way and the way you deal with feedback when you receive it is an important component of creating a safe environment, of building trust, and of showing and receiving respect.

• Are you able to ask for and give open and honest feedback, driven by the strong sense of purpose? Are you able to give feedback to and receive feedback from each other without getting defensive? Are you able to really listen to each other? Are you able to interact with each other without judgment? Are you able to, when necessary, be the "devil's advocate" for each other, and are you able to accept that role from each other? Are you able to set an example in the organization for other people to do the same? Are you, as a team, able to create an environment and an atmosphere in the organization where people feel safe enough to start doing the same? Even if that means going against company politics? Even if, at times, it may mean taking a personal risk?

From the interactions between the members of the team so far (also discussing the questions prior to this one), by now you will have developed a feeling for where people stand individually and as a team. This is the time to discuss that feeling with the people in the team. The way everyone responds will give you and the people in the team a lot of valuable insights.

LEADERSHIP

Respect and Recognition
Customers need to feel respected and valued to create customer advocacy. Employee advocacy precedes customer advocacy. Employees need to feel respected and valued in order to create that same feeling with customers.

- What does respect mean to you? How will it manifest? How do you express the values in real life? How do you react to success? How to failure? Do you respect yourself? Do your employees respect themselves? Are you making respect and recognition tangible for the employees of the company? Are you setting an example? How do you set an example? How do you make respect and recognition tangible?

  Respect and recognition is not in the big things, but in the little things. It's how you deal with people on a day-to-day basis, how you sincerely show interest in them. It's how you make them feel every day. You cannot miss a beat. When you have a "bad hair day," it's your problem, not theirs. Don't make it theirs, but respect yourself, ask yourself why you are having a bad hair day and what you need to do yourself to change it. Don't try to hide it, be open and honest about it. Don't make other people suffer for it. Gandhi said: "Be the change you want to see in the world." It's having gone through these kinds of transformational processes that has made me realize what Gandhi meant. When people don't authentically care about the strong sense of purpose they say they share, people will notice. It will make them feel the opposite of respect and recognition, it will make them feel manipulated, and it will backfire.

A Safe Environment
When you understand and are truly committed to the first five leadership conditions, you're virtually done. But in order to successfully transform an organization into one

that is sustainably able to create employee and customer advocacy, a safe environment requires one last thing. It requires the people responsible for the transformation to be very clear about who's taking the responsibility and the risks. Make it heard time and again, known by all people involved, and shown when and where necessary that you are the one taking the responsibility and the risks, be it your bonus or your job.

So I'm asking you:

• Are you able to create a safe environment for the people in the organization to become engaged in this transformation by openly, fully and completely taking responsibility and claiming the risks involved yourself, even if that means the risk of losing your job, your bonus or your face?

The answers you give/get will speak for themselves.

When you hunger for more questions to ask, a book where you will find many more is Gary Hamel's latest book, *The Future of Management*,[34] about management innovation.

Conclusion

Now that you have an idea how to make the transformation happen that enables organizations to start creating customer advocacy and make it stick, I can imagine that you wonder if your organization can handle such a big change. But the question is, is it such a BIG change? Is it a big change to go back to what's at the core of every human being? Nobody is born with a desire to cover up. Nobody is born with a desire to either hide something or put the blame on someone else. Those are some of the many traits we develop to survive. When we are young, in some cases it can be real survival. As we grow older, it's what society has taught us we need to do to survive and advance in life.

If the people who are managing organizations can take these steps:

- Showing true leadership, whereby people in organizations migrate from surviving in the organization to creating an environment in which they can thrive as the human being they are;
- From managing from industrial paradigms focused on control, to leadership based on setting an example, creating a strong sense of purpose, creating a compelling connective quality with trust, respect, recognition, autonomy, distributing accountability, and creating a safe environment for the people in an organization;
- Creating the kind of environment where people, independent of formal positions, engage each other and raise one another to higher levels of motivation, commitment, responsibility, quality, and performance;

they have made the biggest step. And that's the biggest challenge on the road to employee and customer advocacy.

From Dreams to Feasible Reality

How do you move from intentions and a strong sense of purpose to a differentiating value proposition? How do you identify the ambition level this transformation represents for your company?

IN THE PREVIOUS chapters, I addressed how external and internal changes create the sense of urgency for companies to find new ways to differentiate themselves and create value for customers and employees. I addressed the leadership framework. In this chapter I will add two perspectives, "outside-in" and "inside-out," to give you more of an idea how you can move from dreams and a strong sense of purpose to a differentiating value proposition.

Outside-In

"It's obvious that, to be able to formulate these dreams, people need to know what it is that would make employees and customers want to tell it to the world" (Chapter 4).

To be able to know *"what it is that would make customers want to tell it to the world,"* you need to add a different perspective: the "outside-in" perspective. This makes employees aware of the perception your customers have of your company. The people in your company need to know how customers feel as a result of their interactions with you and how that affects customer behavior.

When you read that, I can imagine you were thinking, *Yes, well, but how? Are we talking traditional market research? Or customer satisfaction research?* Yes, market and customer research is obviously the way to find out, but not in traditional ways.

To start with the latter, I never was a strong advocate of customer satisfaction research. What does it actually tell you to know that x% of your customers are satisfied, and x% are unsatisfied? Not a whole lot, if you ask me. It only starts to become meaningful when you know what the drivers are for (dis-) satisfaction. Even then, customer satisfaction doesn't have a lot of value when you realize that 100% satisfied customers can leave you tomorrow if an alternative comes around. That's why I realized it is more useful to know not just how satisfied customers are but also how committed they are to a company and what makes them committed. Also, this only becomes meaningful when you know it on a regular basis so you can make it actionable. Quarterly or lower frequency research is nice to have, but by the time you get the results, it's hard to make it actionable. You need the ongoing ability to turn the right dial in an operational environment. To make research meaningful, you need a **thermometer** in the operation that tells you on a daily or weekly basis what it is that makes customers committed (and advocates) and what does not. That tells employees what they need to improve where. The changes can be tested immediately, and if the results improve where required, employees know they're on the right track. The only result to get reported at a top management level is likely to be one KPI, such as NPS. The pile of information on top of which that KPI sits is needed and used by the operational people within your organization.

FROM DREAMS TO FEASIBLE REALITY

Traditional market research and competitive analysis can be useful, but more as background information for desk research.

In addition to a thermometer, the people in your company need to develop a feeling for, what Gerald and Lindsay Zaltman in their latest book *Marketing Metaphoria*[35] call, "the deep metaphors" ("*...deep metaphors and emotions are unconscious operations that are vital perceptual and cognitive functions. ... deep metaphors and emotions are universal. ... people experience them at the same basic level worldwide.*"— page 13) and emotions that are specific to consumers and customers buying your category of products and services. There are different ways to execute this kind of research. The most effective way is to involve employees from different departments and different levels of your organization. Confront them with consumers and customers telling them personally what they feel, preferably in a real life setting. Show the guts to ask customers to give feedback and have an interactive dialogue with customers. By involving people that way, it's not a paper tiger you read behind your desk and move aside. When you hear consumers and customers say it in your face it becomes something you feel yourself. The outside-in perspective is necessary to identify what it will take to turn customers into advocates.

INSPIRATIONAL FRAMEWORK

"*Translated into a value proposition, this* [the abundance of choice consumers have, which is confusing to many consumers] *offers a lot of opportunities to create intangible features, or better, benefits, with which companies can differentiate themselves from their competitors. Consumers feel everyone offers the same. The challenge is to design a value proposition that can help a brand become a brand experience*" (Chapter 2).

With the outside-in perspective, you can start to create an inspirational framework that is meaningful to employees. An inspirational framework integrates the value proposition and its benefits into a framework that is intended to inspire employees to create experiences that are meaningful to customers.

The strong sense of purpose and the dreams I addressed in Chapter 4 remain the point of reference. The inspirational framework makes it tangible, it describes the garden and its boundaries (Chapter 4, 'Autonomy'), and gives employees clues for how to create meaningful experiences (emotional endframe) for customers.

Inside-Out

In order to successfully execute a transformational process to create customer advocacy, you need to know the level of ambition this transformation actually represents with respect to the current status of your organization. The inside-out perspective is a reality check to assess the organizational maturity with respect to the ability to create employee and customer advocacy.

STRATEGY

Are the vision and strategy of your company aligned with creating customer advocacy? Is there a "strong sense of purpose" that is shared among all the employees of your company, from top to bottom?

There are multiple examples to be found in the online world, but let's stick to one company. Let's have a look at the basics of Amazon.com.[36]

Their "strong sense of purpose" is: "Earth's Most Customer-Centric Company."

This strong sense of purpose is backed up by their "Amazon Values":

"We make decisions as a company, and as individuals, based on our core values."

Their core values are:

- *Customer Obsession:* We start with the customer and work backwards.
- *Innovation:* If you don't listen to your customers you will fail. But if you only listen to your customers you will also fail.
- *Bias for Action:* We live in a time of unheralded revolution and insurmountable opportunity—provided we make every minute count.
- *Ownership:* Ownership matters when you're building a great company. Owners think long-term, plead passionately for their projects and ideas, and are empowered to respectfully challenge decisions.
- *High Hiring Bar:* When making a hiring decision we ask ourselves: "Will I admire this person? Will I learn from this person? Is this person a superstar?
- *Frugality:* We spend money on things that really matter and believe that frugality breeds resourcefulness, self-sufficiency, and invention!

I leave it up to you, as a reader, who undoubtedly had experiences with Amazon as a customer, to remember how you felt as a result of doing business with Amazon and how your feelings relate to their strong sense of purpose and core values (see chapter 1).

By now, you should be able to assess to what extent the vision and strategy of your company have been translated into a strong sense of purpose that is shared among all the employees, from top to bottom, creating a "compelling connective quality" for all employees in your company and a meaningful environment for all stakeholders, especially employees and customers. And, you should know how ambitious it will be to create it, if that isn't the case today.

STRUCTURE

As I said in the first chapter, creating employee and customer advocacy requires a high level organizational design that is first and foremost customer-driven. It requires an environment where the people working in your organization are empowered to take ownership and responsibility themselves. Let's go back to the example of Amazon, and their core values.

"Customer Obsession: We start with the customer and work backwards."

"Innovation: If you don't listen to your customers you will fail. But if you only listen to your customers you will also fail."

Both core values illustrate a high level organizational design that is customer-driven.

"Ownership: Ownership matters when you're building a great company. Owners think long-term, plead passionately for their projects and ideas, and are empowered to respectfully challenge decisions."

Amazon is a striking illustration of an environment where the employees are empowered to take ownership and responsibility themselves.

The more your company is an industrial age, controllable machine, hierarchically organized, and silo-ed, the more ambitious the transformation will be and the more time and energy you will need to invest in awareness, development, and buy-in of the individual people, especially at the top of the pyramid. Probably you will only be able to be successful if the financial results of the company have been suffering and the sense of urgency is growing every day. You will need to choose the right moment, over and over again, and you will need patience.

GOVERNANCE

Governance related to creating employee and customer advocacy requires the highest level of "walking the talk" possible, consistently setting an example through your own behavior, and creating policies and processes that are consistent with the goal of creating employee and customer advocacy.

Going back to the core values of Amazon:

"Ownership: Ownership matters when you're building a great company. Owners think long-term, plead passionately for their projects and ideas, and are empowered to respectfully challenge decisions."

This core value says a lot about the way the governance of Amazon works. They emphasize ownership, they regard their employees as owners, and they emphasize the behavior and decision-right that goes with ownership.

What are the decision-rights of the people working for your company based on? Are they based on a corporate-governance doctrine, which forcibly pushes people into policies and processes? What is the behavior of the board and their like? Do they walk the talk? What example do you set? You need to take all this into account in your assessment of your company.

PERFORMANCE MANAGEMENT

Employee and customer advocacy requires performance management that sets the kind of goals that create advocacy and rewards the achievement of these goals.

"Bias for Action: We live in a time of unheralded revolution and insurmountable opportunity—provided we make every minute count."

"Frugality: We spend money on things that really matter and believe that frugality breeds resourcefulness, self-sufficiency, and invention!"

The basis for the performance management within Amazon is embedded in their core values.

- Make every minute count
- Be resourceful
- Be self-sufficient
- Be inventive

What you need to be looking for is quite banal. What are things like remuneration, bonuses, and promotions based on? If it's all financial (quarterly, yearly; operating cashflow; revenue; EBITDA; etc.) and driven by being successful in company politics, the gap is bound to be large and the challenge starts at the top.

PROCESSES AND SYSTEMS

The focus for processes in a company that sets out to create advocacy should be enabling employees and customers to improve the outcome for its customers, improve the convenience of doing business with that company, increase the level of control, and help customers (and employees) deal with the abundance of choices they have. You need to offer a customer the best solution your company has to offer, in ways that suit your customer the best, in the best conditions. You need to offer employees the tools that enable them to adequately support the customers they serve and balance customer and company interests.

Amazon is one of the first and probably best examples of how to deploy processes and systems to that purpose. What will be quite telling is how decisions to invest in systems in your company are made, how processes are developed, and what role the processes play in the configuration and implementation of systems. Which departments are actively involved, and at what phases of the process?

The ambition level for the transformation gets higher as:

- Decisions to invest in systems are driven more by the IT department and/or procurement, without active involvement of the business side of the organization (marketing, sales, operations);
- Systems are based more on the technical specifications of the IT department than the functional requirements of the business;
- Implementations and migrations are less tested and issues solved more after the go-live date;
- Processes are more re-engineered based on the technical specifications of the system, driven by what the system can offer than what the business requires;
- User acceptance testing is more defined by user cases defined by the IT department than by the business side of the organization;
- Training is more the part of the roadmap that gets squeezed (time and budget-wise) between testing and the desire to stick to the communicated go-live date.

CAPABILITIES, BEHAVIOR AND LEADERSHIP

Capabilities, behavior and leadership need to be consistent with the goal of creating employee and customer advocacy. The people within your organization need to have the right character (the inner values that make the environment meaningful to them as a human being; Chapter 7), the right competencies, and show the right behavior and leadership style to make advocacy happen. Apart from the walk-the-talk perspective, which is probably clear by now, let's go to the core values of Amazon one more time.

"High Hiring Bar: When making a hiring decision we ask ourselves: 'Will I admire this person? Will I learn from this person? Is this person a superstar?'"

This core value says a lot not just about the kind of people Amazon hires, but maybe even more about the people who work for Amazon. What does it tell you about the capabilities, the behavior and the leadership style of people working for Amazon if they view their (future) co-workers this way? Yes, a company needs people with the right skills to be successful. But when a company wants to create advocacy, it also needs people with the right character. As Howard Schultz from Starbucks said, "You can train people to make coffee, not how to smile." Stephen Covey[37] defines character as integrity and intent (Chapter 3). The authenticity of the people representing an organization, from top to bottom is the most critical success factor for creating sustainable advocacy. People at all levels of an organization need to set an example, show integrity, and be open and honest about their intent, about their own truth, and about their own values, which need to be consistent with the company values and appeal to your customers. So, you need to assess the character, the capabilities, the behavior, and the leadership style of your company in order to get an idea of the level of ambition this part of the equation represents.

Executing this reality check will give you guidance to assess the level of ambition to transform the company to one that is capable of creating advocacy and to develop roadmaps for those areas where inconsistencies have been identified.

Conclusion

The two perspectives, outside-in and inside-out, will give you a clear picture of: how you can move from dreams to reality; how your company can differentiate itself from its competitors in ways that are relevant (customers), credible (brand) and unique (competitors) to a level that will create customer advocacy; how to translate it into a framework that is inspiring and aspiring for the people in your organization; and what the organizational hurdles are that you need to address to make the transformation successful and the creation of advocacy really happen.

Customer Advocacy and Bottom Line Impact

Customer advocacy may sound soft but it isn't. On the contrary, the budget required to create it is lower than the amount of money companies tend to invest in traditional marketing. The returns are higher and more tangible than those made through traditional marketing.

CUSTOMERS AND EMPLOYEES are usually categorized as intangible assets. The highest investment customer advocacy requires is in those intangible assets–customers and employees. Financial statements usually don't contain much information about these intangible assets.

In most organizations, 80% of the management time and attention is directed at the tangible assets of a company and only 20% at the intangible assets.[38] Companies don't calculate the growth potential of their customer base, they just state a growth target based on– what? A competitive analysis, a market analysis, all kinds of external and internal drivers. More often than not, the announced growth target for companies is peanuts if you compare it to the size, hence the growth potential, of their customer base. But because companies are not used to seeing their customer base as a tangible asset, they don't value the quality of it or the growth potential it can represent. If, however, the level of customer advocacy among a customer base is high, it says not only something about its quality but about its growth potential and the true growth potential of a company. This potential can increase profits, because as markets become saturated, products and services commoditized and companies are confronted with hyper-competition, growth through new sales becomes harder to achieve and so expensive that it is harder to be profitable. Companies lose their existing customers because they focus all their attention on acquiring new customers, neglecting the ones they already have.

Fred Reichheld has executed a lot of research to investigate the relationship between the NPS and profitable growth. He concluded that there's a profound correlation between the NPS and the profitable growth potential of companies.[39]

Investments

The investments required to make a transformation happen in an organization that will enable the organization to create customer advocacy are not so much counted in money as in:

- The willingness and belief of people, starting at the top, to take personal risks, to invest in the process themselves as human beings, and set an example. (By now, I hope that by what you read in this book so far I have been able to give you an idea about these dimensions.); and
- Time and patience. Customer advocacy is not something that can be achieved overnight. It's not something that will help jazz up next quarters' performance. Depending on the existing culture of an organization, it can take from half a year up to several years to implement.

The investment in money can be as high or as low as companies allow. But any investment is throwing good money after bad if the people in the company don't take personal risks, invest in the process themselves as human beings, and set an example. Companies can spend a lot of money on internal communication programs, but if people in an organization are not triggered to add to the process from their own creativity (think of the garden I described) to come up with their own contributions and take ownership and responsibility, it will be throwing good money after bad. When people in an organization start to brainstorm about how they can add to the transformation during their lunch breaks and at the coffee machine, that's when you'll see real change starting to happen. If they then ask you for some money to execute their initiative, for instance to have funny T-shirts made, you should jump at the occasion. However, especially with Generation Y, if management would come up with that same idea and distribute those funny T-shirts, would they wear them? You would probably be mocked and find your T-shirts in the recycling bin.

You should also come up with creative ways, or better yet, create space for the people in the organization to come up with ideas to celebrate successes. It can be as easy as surprising people on the work floor with a day to celebrate their stardom, laying out a red carpet and have the management welcome them at the door in the morning, serve them coffee, cake, lunch, thee, the works during that day as they set out to serve customers. Make them feel what it feels like to be respected and valued for what they do.

I do have to make one reservation. Customer advocacy cannot be build on a wobbly frame. By that, I mean companies who want to deploy the opportunities of customer advocacy as the next competitive battleground do need to have achieved a level of operational excellence and product leadership, at least to the degree that the quality of their products and services as well as their operational efficiency are demonstrably up to par. The investment picture looks rather different if a company has not achieved that as a minimum level, but then, it is debatable if customer advocacy would be the right strategy for them anyway.

Return on Investment

As you have seen, the investment money-wise doesn't have to be extravagant, but in time, patience, guts, persistence, perseverance, creativity and personal commitment, it is. Once an organization starts to create employee advocacy, customer advocacy will follow. Once customer advocacy starts to show a positive trend:

- Employee sickness ratios will have decreased;
- Employee turnover will have decreased;
- Recruitment costs will have decreased;
- Customer acquisition costs will decrease;
- Cost to serve will decrease;
- Cross- and up-selling will increase;
- Profitability of the company will increase;
- And at some point you're bound to see a positive impact on the share price, too.

In Chapter 7, you will find an overview of the KPI's to make employee and customer advocacy tangible, measurable, and sustainable (the Customer Advocacy Monitor).

Conclusion

Customer advocacy is simple, but not easy. It's like a New Year's resolution. On New Year's Eve, you absolutely belief that's what you want to do and that you can do it. You set your goal of losing twenty pounds. But what happens after you've lost the first ten? Will you lose your perspective and adjust your goal? What will you do when the going gets tough?

The investment to create customer advocacy is relatively low on the cost-side. The highest investment is the willingness, the belief, the persistence, and the perseverance of people, starting at the top, to take personal risks, to invest in the process themselves as human beings, and to set an example, not to mention time and patience. That's what makes it one of the toughest transformations, especially for companies that are managed and have been managed for decades by industrial-age paradigms.

The positive bottom line impact potential of customer advocacy is high on the cost-side *and* on the revenue-side. What's maybe most important, it's not a quick fix, but it does create a sustainable competitive advantage that cannot be copied by competitors. Your competitors might beat you to it, though.

7

How to Make Customer Advocacy Sustainable?

Companies need to make customer advocacy a sustainable competitive advantage to create profitable, organic growth. Therefore, it needs to be financially accountable and measurable, and your actions must be continuously aligned with changing customer desires and values.

USTAINABILITY IS A key word here, both from a customer and a company perspective. Sustainability means customers build up preference, loyalty and commitment to a brand and/or a company. Sustainability starts with doing the right things and becomes permanent by doing things right. Along these lines, I will describe two kinds of measurement: the Customer Advocacy Indicator (doing the right things) and the Customer Advocacy Monitor (doing things right). I will try to give you an inside view of what these do. The Customer Advocacy Monitor especially will give you an idea how employee and customer advocacy impact the financial performance of a company.

WHEN YOU CARE, PEOPLE NOTICE

Customer Advocacy Indicator

"Companies need to profile the values, ethics, culture and behaviors of the people in their organization against their business objectives, and their customers or customer segments. If employee and customer advocacy is part of your business, you need to start with making sure that the inner values, ethics, culture and behaviors of all the people from top to bottom within your organization are adequate to do the job." (Chapter 3).

The Customer Advocacy Indicator is a way to assess the inner values and value systems of your employees and your customers. The output can be used: to define how you can transform the environment your organization embodies into one that is meaningful for both employees and customers; to identify the gaps between employees working in different departments and layers; to identify the gaps between the environment within your organization and the outside world (i.e., customers or customer segments); to find clues to optimize the interactions among your employees, and between them and your customers; to guide the softer side of the transformation in the initial phase of the process and assess the development along the way; and to continuously align your actions with the changing customer desires and values.

You would like to know which segments of your customers are actively promoting your brands, products, and services and which are shaping your business on a moment-by-moment basis. While customer advocacy is day-to-day behavior resulting from a complex of dynamic processes, you are even more interested in how to optimize the conditions and tune management processes to achieve high impact through customer advocacy. From a leadership perspective, a reliable forecast and a clear roadmap on how to achieve significant strategic impact through customer advocacy is even more important than contemplating the data of the actual situation.

Company leaders have indicated they would be interested in having a robust, reliable method to identify the statistical chance that customers—in autonomous, authentic, spontaneous, and proactive ways—tell positive stories about the company and its brands, products and services. More than fifteen years of scientific research have been combined with pragmatic business experience to design the strategic framework to predict whether customers will act as active ambassadors. This framework has been called the Customer Advocacy Indicator (CAI).

The underlying theory of the CAI assumes that, when customers are connecting with employees of the company, if they are treated in respectful, warm ways that are important to that individual customer, this may open the heart of the customer to start telling positive stories spontaneously.

In practice, the CAI is a suite of dedicated tools and methods enabling a match between the values and behavioral attitudes of employees with the respective customers. It is the degree of matching that gives a predictive indication of customer advocacy.

Large-scale improvement projects are driven by a gap-to-fill approach: the gap of the matching between customers and employees may be filled by either large-scale employee development projects and/or a new way of value-based organizing, in which specific groups of employees are focused on serving customer segments closely matching the employee group's values profile.

Customer Advocacy Monitor

The KPIs to create a zero level measurement and keep track of the trends and developments to verify if your company is on the right track in creating customer advocacy centers around four key areas: the customer's value perception; the customer's brand perception; the relationship perception[40] of your customers; and the advocacy of your employees.

VALUE PERCEPTION

To measure the impact on the value perception from a customer perspective, you need to measure:

1) Share of wallet
   a) Cross- and up-selling
   b) Recency, frequency and monetary value
   c) Customer lifetime value

Data on customers who spend more money with your company more frequently, who spend more money altogether, and who remain customers longer is a tangible way to verify if your company is creating a balance between quality and price in the perception of its customers. When a customer keeps coming back for more, he's showing through his behavior that he likes doing business with you.

To measure the impact on the value perception from a company perspective, you need to measure:

2) Profitability
   a) Operational efficiency
   b) Cost to serve
   c) Margins
   d) Development of the share price

The expression used to be: "Profit is the reward of a satisfied customer." Not anymore. Profit nowadays is the reward of a loyal customer, who is engaged to a level of advocacy. From an internal perspective, you can tell if you are turning the right dials when the operational efficiency increases and the cost to serve decreases. These trends tell something about customers' perception of the convenience of doing business with your company and their level of trust in your employees. When these trends are improving, it is fair to assume that in the perception of your customers it is becoming easier to do business with your company. Remember, the lower the trust, the lower the speed and the higher the cost.[41] The lower the level of customer trust, the more frequently they will contact you. When a customer keeps coming back for more, the margins improve because your company has to make less of an effort to sell to that customer, not to mention that an advocate does the selling for you through positive word-of-mouth (traditional, online and CGM), attracting new customers. Therefore these trends will also translate to an improvement in the margins of your company, providing profitable (organic) growth. At some point, this will have a positive effect on the share price as well.

BRAND PERCEPTION

To measure the impact on the brand perception from a customer perspective, you need to measure:

3) Brand awareness
4) Reputation of the brand
5) Positioning of the brand

The fact that consumers know your company (brand) is not by definition positive. The question is, what is the attitude of customers towards the brand? When customers speak highly of your brand, that's when their perception is moving into the right direction and your company is on the right track. But what is "speaking highly of your brand"? What is the perception of the ethics of your brand, and how do these compare to customers' own ethics? When the ethics of your brand don't match up with the ethics of your customers, you may be fooling yourself. What looks like a positive development may not be sustainable. If you have a mismatch with respect to the ethics of your brand and those of the customer, your customer will find out one day and is likely to take her business to a competitor where she does find (or thinks she will find) that match.

The better the match between the positioning of your brand and the perception of your customers and the more successfully your company matches the communicated value proposition with the value proposition as it is delivered to and perceived by your customers, the higher the likelihood of customers telling it to the world-spreading the news to others as well.

To measure the impact on the brand perception from a company perspective, you need to measure:

6) Competitiveness of the brand
7) Brand value

One of the key strategic reasons to start creating customer advocacy is to create a sustainable competitive advantage that is hard to copy. It is key to keep track of the competitiveness of your brand and to verify frequently how customers perceive your brand comparing to the competition. The brand value represents a longer-term effect, which should start to show a positive trend over time. How much time depends on several factors, such as the value and the reputation of your brand at the start of the transformational process (both internally with the people working for your company, and externally with consumers and your customers). But it also depends on the competitive playing field. If your brand is facing a strong competitor with a high level of preference, loyalty and commitment from its customers, it will be a lot harder to convince those consumers to switch and for you to claim this position in the marketplace. That in itself is a factor you need to take into account when deciding on a strategy focused on customer advocacy.

RELATIONSHIP PERCEPTION

To measure the impact on the relationship perception from a customer perspective, you need to measure:

8) Churn/retention
9) Customer satisfaction
10) Customer advocacy (Net Promoter Score)

The strength of the relationship with your customers says something about their relationship perception. When you lose customers (churn), it is key to know what made those customers leave. It is possible that a customer might have high levels of preference, loyalty, and commitment, and still leave. Think for instance about a company that sells diapers. As soon as the last baby in a family is potty trained, it's unlikely that this customer will continue to buy diapers. But in most cases it is not as clear cut as that. It is especially in those cases where a customer has switched to a competitor where you need to know what made a customer decide to end the relationship.

Think about a bank that starts to lose a lot of its customers, some of whom have been with that bank their whole life. Chances are that a lot of customers decided to switch because they found an alternative that offered them a better value proposition. For instance, it offers them integrated packages that combine traditional banking, online banking, mobile banking, telephone banking, text message banking, mortgages, loans, credit cards, savings, investments, share dealing, insurances, and travel services, and a personal advisor who knows a customers' situation, his likes and dislikes, his preferences. The personal advisor proactively advises the customer when he can get a better interest on his savings accounts, keeps track of account balances, and knows what a customer's preferences are when he initiates a share deal that overrides his account balance. The advisor knows when the customer's paycheck is due, so he arranges a temporary loan because the adviser knows that is what the customer prefers. And so on, and so forth. The customer knows that this is a value proposition his traditional bank cannot offer him. Also, he heard many people speak highly of this alternative. His research on the Web checked out. Although the customer doesn't like leaving the bank where he has been a longtime customer, he decided to switch. Granted, this may seem like a quite extraordinary example, but these are the kinds of scenarios happening in all kinds of industries. What's even more worrisome, in many cases the alternatives are international players entering a local market or new market entrants full stop. So, it is not only the KPI you need to know, but also what is behind it and what caused it.

Customer satisfaction precedes customer advocacy, and it's important to know what the drivers of both are. What is driving customer (dis-)satisfaction is key information for the operational people within your company, because more often than not, it is things happening on the operational side, unless, of course, the quality of products or services is not good enough. In both cases, it is important to have teams, preferably multi-disciplinary, dealing with the drivers for dissatisfaction to address these as adequately and as quickly as possible. Have these teams come up with a funky name for themselves, empower them, and make them visible in the organization. For instance, the name one of the teams I worked with gave themselves was "Booster-team." With each issue they solved, they saw the impact on the customer satisfaction and the customer advocacy, and their engagement, eagerness to solve problems, and pride grew.

Hence my statement: *"The pile of information on top of which that KPI sits is needed and used by the operational people of your organization"* (Chapter 5). I hope that you now understand that customer satisfaction scores and a KPI that represents the customer advocacy (be it NPS or another KPI) are just the tip of the iceberg. At a top-management level these scores are sufficient to observe the trends, but at an operational level they aren't. Reichheld's NPS is, in my experience, the best way to translate customer advocacy into one KPI. But asking "the ultimate question" ("Would you recommend this company to your family and friends?") is not enough. If you don't know what's driving the answer, you can't know what you need to do to make the needle move. Therefore, here too, it's important to know what drives it. And even then, it is also important to track what customers say about your brand in online and off-line environments, and to deal with the answers on the one hand by addressing allegations appropriately (fitting the ethics of the medium), and on the other hand by learning from of it and addressing the appropriate parts of your organization.

To measure the impact on the relationship perception from a company perspective, you need to measure:

11) Touch point conversion
12) Customer Acquisition Cost

The internal perspective on the relationship perception of your customers can, indirectly, be inferred from the trends you see with respect to the touch point conversion and the Customer Acquisition Cost. In the cases I worked on, for example, the conversion of customer service went from, in many cases, next to nothing, to becoming the largest sales channel (while the cost to serve went down and the operational efficiency increased). Customer service in those cases was also the cheapest sales channel, so the Customer Acquisition Cost went down materially as well. You can imagine what that did to the margins.

EMPLOYEE ADVOCACY

That leaves one key area to be addressed, which is the employee advocacy. As said, employee advocacy precedes customer advocacy. It is important that you measure consistently and structurally (i.e., more frequent than once or twice a year) the following KPIs with respect to employees:

a) Employee satisfaction
b) Employee advocacy (Employee Net Promoter Score)
c) Employee sickness ratios (both short- and long-term sickness)
d) Employee turnover
e) Recruitment cost

Remember what I said about the Booster-team? With each issue they solved, they saw the impact they had on customer satisfaction and customer advocacy, and their engagement, eagerness to solve problems, and pride grew. What I said earlier about customer satisfaction and customer advocacy is also applicable to employee satisfaction and employee advocacy. Here, too, the devil is in the details. It's not just knowing the KPI, but also what causes the performance on the KPI that enables you to improve the score. Obviously, when you see a positive trend of these two KPIs, you should also see it translated into a positive trend of the employee sickness ratios and the employee turnover. Employees who are advocates for your company experience a high level of wellbeing and are less likely to report in sick or leave your company. Unless, again, there's a desire or wish your company cannot fulfill.

As the employee and customer advocacy pick up, it will become easier for your company to attract employees, because the reputation of your company travels ahead and does its work also in this area. So, at some point in the process, you should see the recruitment cost show a downward trend, too.

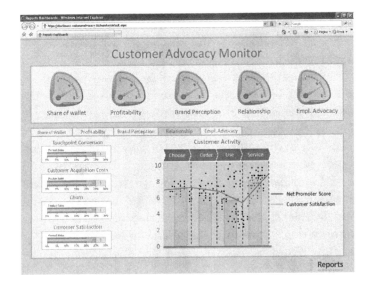

Conclusion

The Customer Advocacy Indicator is a way to assess the core of your organization, i.e., the inner values and value systems of employees; and to assess the inner values and value systems of the customer. It is a way to guide the softer side of the transformation in the initial phase of the process, assess the development along the way, and continuously align your actions with the changing customer desires and values. The Customer Advocacy Indicator represents a strategic framework based on more than fifteen years of scientific research combined with pragmatic operational business experience to predict the probability that customers will act as active ambassadors.

The Customer Advocacy Monitor is a way to measure the impact of employee and customer advocacy on the financial performance of your company; a way to make it financially accountable and measurable.

Most of the suggested KPIs are already measured and reported in most companies. Bringing them together into one Customer Advocacy dashboard supplies you with the overview you need to be able to manage it. What isn't visible at the dashboard level is all the additional information gathered to calculate these KPIs. The KPIs are the tip of the iceberg, and the operational people within your organization need to be enabled to see both these KPIs and the whole of the iceberg to be able to understand which buttons to push and which dials to turn to take ownership and responsibility for the improvement of the perceptions of employees and customers. Seeing is believing. Seeing their (i.e., the operational people in your organization) impact on these KPIs and realizing through the iceberg how they impact them, employees' engagement, eagerness, commitment, and pride will grow. That's why it's so important in order to be successful at creating customer advocacy to create an open and honest culture where there are no unwritten rules, no company politics, and no hiding, because nothing is hidden, hence there's nothing to hide behind.

I hope that I have made it clear how profitability in today's environment depends on customer advocacy, which in turn depends on employee advocacy. As a side effect, what I recommend will also make for great corporate environments, thereby reducing stress and making families stronger.

One last word of warning. If the people who set out to make this kind of transformation happen are driven by ego, don't even think of starting. Because in order for it to be successful, each individual person in the organization, no matter what level they operate on, needs to feel that it's his success too.

About the author

NICOLETTE WURING HAS become a thought leader in this domain not through academic research, but through hands-on experience at inspiring transformations within large multinational organizations that transformed employees into advocates, who in turn transformed customers into advocates. This led to sustainable material improvements of the financial performance of these companies.

Nicolette is the former Vice President, Customer Care for UPC Broadband Europe, a 10+ million customer Multi System (Cable) Operator active in eleven countries in Western and Central Europe, where she was responsible for the turnaround of the customer facing side of its business from worst in class to best in class for servicing its customers, winning two Contact Center Awards and a nomination for the CRM Award.

Service has become one of the key differentiators of UPC Broadband; the cost to serve and the customer acquisition costs decreased materially; the customer loyalty as well as the share of wallet increased significantly.

Nicolette has a long, successful history in the field of Customer Operations. She has been responsible for launching services such as pay-per-view, pay-TV, high speed data, cable telephony and e-services as well as mergers and reorganizations in various companies and countries in Europe and the U.S.

Her background as a classical singer and a scientist in music have been instrumental in her thought-provoking approach to business. She is tuned into what's happening in society and the way the two are related – the way music, and the arts in general, always are closely connected to and impacted by what's happening in society, as well as the inescapable creativity with which they reflect on and respond to society.

Nicolette is the founder and managing director of Customer M@nagement Services, a strategic consulting company that specializes in creating and implementing value and service propositions that increase companies' brand equity, bottom line performance, as well as inspire their employees and customers to a level of engagement and advocacy. Her passion is assisting, guiding and inspiring companies in their strategic reorientation and transformation from shareholder- to stakeholder-driven; from product-driven to people-driven.

She also facilitates:

Transformational Leadership Programs that assist leaders in their personal growth, transforming the way they operate and manage themselves and others from being driven externally to their own essence from *human doing* to *human being*; to becoming people who, independent of formal positions, engage people in such a way that they raise one another to higher levels of motivation, commitment, responsibility, quality and performance.

Employee and Customer Advocacy Master Classes, a program that introduces business people, marketers, service people, and others to the essence of transformational leadership, engagement, loyalty and advocacy of employees and customers.

Feedback

I F THE CONTENT of this book has triggered a desire in you to give me your feedback, share with me your story, or get in touch with me, please do so.

You can send me an e-mail at nicolette@ customeradvocacy.biz, and I will be happy to get back to you within 24 hours.

Thank you for investing your time, first of all in reading this book, and should you decide to contact me, for taking the time to do so.

Feel free to quote from this book. I would appreciate it if you mention the source when doing so.

May you leave these pages inspired and eager to get at it in your own life, as well as the life of the people you work with, be it your co-workers or your customers!

References

- Manfred Kets de Vries, 2000, *The Happiness Equation*
- Bourne, M., Franco, M. and Wilkes, J., 2003, *Corporate performance management. Measuring Business Excellence*
- Eric Harvey and Steve Ventura, 2007, *Walk the Talk* (www.WalkTheTalk.com)
- Ken Blanchard and Barbara Glanz, 2005, *The Simple Truths of Service* (www.simpletruths.com)
- Chris Anderson, Random House Business Books, 2006, *The Long Tail. How Endless Choice is Creating Unlimited Demand*
- Rust, Zeithaml and Lemon, *Customer Equity: How Customer Lifetime Value is Reshaping Corporate Strategy*
- Fred Reichheld, 2006, Harvard Business School Press, *The Ultimate Question: Would you recommend this company to your family and friends*
- Boschma and Groen, 2006, *Generatie Einstein*
- *Financial Times*, 20 September 2006, Digital Business, "They are the future. And they're coming soon to a workplace near you."
- Lewis P. Carbone, FT Press, 2004, *Clued In*
- Gary Hamel with Bill Breen, 2007, Harvard Business School Press, *The Future of Management*

- Stephen M.R. Covey, 2006, *The Speed of Trust*
- Gerald Zaltman and Lindsay H. Zaltman, 2008, Harvard Business Press, *Marketing Metaphoria; What Deep Metaphors Reveal About The Minds of Consumers*
- Chris Zook, 2007, *Unstoppable. Finding Hidden Assets to Renew the Core and Fuel Profitable Growth*
- Fijlstra and Wullings, 2004, *Honesty, the Best Policy*
- Professor Wessel Ganzevoort, Titus Brandsma lecture, 2003: *Spirituality in leadership*
- Interview with Paul de Bloth, Financeel Dagblad, the Netherlands, July 19, 2007
- Glen L. Urban, Alfred P. Sloan School of Management, Massachusetts Institute of Technology (MIT), 2003, *The Trust Imperative*
- Kevin Roberts, CEO Worldwide Saatchi & Saatchi (www.saatchikevin.com)
- Jhon P. Strelecky, 2008, St. Martin's Press, *The Big Five For Live; A Story of One Man and Leadership's Greatest Secret*
- Rajendra S. Sisodia, David B. Wolfe, Jagdish N. Sheth, 2007, Wharton School Publishing, *Firms of Endearment: How World-Class Companies Profit from Passion and Purpose*

Endnotes

1. Ken Blanchard & Barbara Glanz, 2005, *The Simple Truths of Service* (www.simpletruths.com)
2. The Conference Board, *CEO Challenge 2007, Top 10 Challenges, Research Report R-1406-07-RR*
3. Boschma & Groen, 2006, *Generatie Einstein*
4. Inspired by: Rust, Zeithaml and Lemon, Customer Equity: *How Customer Lifetime Value is Reshaping Corporate Strategy*
5. Philip Kotler
6. Manfred Kets de Vries, 2000, *The Happiness Equation*
7. Wikipedia
8. Eric Harvey & Steve Ventura, 2007, *Walk the Talk* (www.WalkTheTalk.com)
9. Bourne, M., Franco, M. and Wilkes, J., 2003, *Corporate performance management. Measuring Business Excellence*
10. J.V. Downtown, 1973, *Rebel Leadership: Commitment and Charisma in a Revolutionary Process*
11. Fred Reichheld, 2006, Harvard Business School Press, *The Ultimate Question: Would you recommend this company to your family and friends*
12. Gary Hamel with Bill Breen, 2007, Harvard Business School Press, *The Future of Management*
13. Chris Anderson, Random House Business Books, 2006, *The Long Tail. How Endless Choice is Creating Unlimited Demand*

14. Kevin Roberts, Chief Executive Officer Worldwide of the advertising agency Saatchi & Saatchi, 2005, Powerhouse Books, *Lovemarks: The Future Beyond Brands*
15. www.lovemarks.com
16. Fred Reichheld, 2006, Harvard Business School Press, *The Ultimate Question: Would you recommend this company to your family and friends*
17. Stephen M.R. Covey, 2006, *The Speed of Trust*
18. *Financial Times*, 20 September 2006, Digital Business, "They are the future. And they're coming soon to a workplace near you."
19. www.monsterboard.com
20. Lewis P. Carbone, FT Press, 2004, *Clued In*
21. Gary Hamel with Bill Breen, 2007, Harvard Business School Press, *The Future of Management*
22. Attributed to Peter Drucker
23. Lewis P. Carbone, FT Press, 2004, *Clued In*
24. Manfred Kets de Vries, Raoul de Vitry d'Avaucourt Chair of Leadership Development at one of Europe's top business schools, Insead, France
25. Manfred Kets de Vries, 2000, *The Happiness Equation*
26. Chris Zook, 2007, *Unstoppable. Finding Hidden Assets to Renew the Core and Fuel Profitable Growth*
27. Towers Perrin, *Winning Strategies for a Global Workplace: Executive Report 2006,* Quoting Gary Hamel with Bill Breen, 2007, Harvard Business School Press, *The Future of Management*
28. *Laweiplein*, Drachten, The Netherlands
29. See Fijlstra and Wullings, 2004, *Honesty, the Best Policy* for a more in-depth description of the progression from the agricultural age to the industrial age to the information age and the transformational age.
30. Wessel Ganzevoort, former Chairman of KPMG Management Consulting Europe, former Vice-Chairman of KPMG Management Consulting Worldwide, now professor of Organization Dynamics and Innovation at

the University of Amsterdam (The Netherlands), Titus Brandsma lecture, 2003: *Spirituality in leadership*

31. Lewis P. Carbone, FT Press, 2004, *Clued In*
32. Interview with Paul de Bloth, Financeel Dagblad, the Netherlands, July 19, 2007
33. Stephen M.R. Covey, 2006, *The Speed of Trust*
34. Gary Hamel with Bill Breen, 2007, Harvard Business School Press, *The Future of Management*
35. Gerald Zaltman and Lindsay H. Zaltman, 2008, Harvard Business Press, *Marketing Metaphoria; What Deep Metaphors Reveal About The Minds of Consumers*
36. www.amazon.com
37. Stephen M.R. Covey, 2006, *The Speed of Trust*
38. Wouter Huibregtsen, former chairman McKinsey Benelux
39. Fred Reichheld, 2006, Harvard Business School Press, *The Ultimate Question: Would you recommend this company to your family and friends*
40. Inspired by: Rust, Zeithaml and Lemon, Customer Equity: *How Customer Lifetime Value is Reshaping Corporate Strategy*
41. Stephen M.R. Covey, 2006, *The Speed of Trust*

CPSIA information can be obtained at www.ICGtesting.com
Printed in the USA
LVOW070817070312

271984LV00005B/33/P